100 YEARS OF THE ULSTER GRAND PRIX

100 YEARS OF THE

ULSTER GRAND PRIX

A CENTURY OF ROAD RACING

NORMAN WINDRUM

THE BLACKSTAFF PRESS

First published in 2022 by Blackstaff Press
an imprint of Colourpoint Creative Ltd
Colourpoint House
Jubilee Business Park
21 Jubilee Road
Newtownards BT23 4YH

Printed by GPS Colour Graphics Ltd, Belfast

A CIP catalogue for this book is available from the British Library

ISBN 978-1-78073-305-0

www.blackstaffpress.com

CONTENTS

INTRODUCTION

Saturday, 16 August 1947 was a day that, in some respects, shaped the course of my life. That was the date of the first Ulster Grand Prix held after the end of the Second World War.

I was ten years of age at the time, and the week before the race had spent several afternoons and evenings excitedly watching the riders make their way to and from practice as they travelled along the road in Belfast where I lived. In those days, only the 'works' riders and a few of the wealthier 'privateers' had the luxury of vans or trailers; the majority of the competitors actually rode their machines to and from the Clady circuit. It was witnessing this spectacle that prompted me to ask my uncle – or, more accurately, torment him until he agreed – to take me with him to Clady for the race itself.

Getting to the race meant a long walk from the tram terminus at Ligoniel on the outskirts of the city right up over the seemingly never-ending Wolfhill to Clady Corner. But once there, perched near the end of the famous Seven Mile Straight, I found myself mesmerised. Whether it was the speed, the crescendo of noise, the smell of Castrol R, or the excited crowds, I am not sure, but I loved every minute of it and was well and truly hooked.

Now, seventy-five years later, I'm still fortunate enough to watch today's generation of riders, and I still get as excited as I ever did on a Saturday race morning as I load up my car with my rucksack, folding chair, sunblock, and, of course, umbrella. It goes without saying that the Ulster Grand Prix is my favourite race.

In 1979, on the occasion of the 50th Ulster Grand Prix, I wrote a book covering its history, and in the years since then I have been asked many times to update it. The problem, however, is that in the earlier years of the Ulster there were, at most, three races to cover, whereas in recent times this has grown to double figures. To continue the story in the same style from 1978 (where my last book ended) would have led to a disjointed and, indeed, somewhat boring narrative.

This time, therefore, I decided to tell the story of 'the Ulster' in a different way; by concentrating on the actual development of the race, and what went on at times behind the scenes. I realise, of course, that readers will still want to read about the riders who graced the roads of Clady and Dundrod over the years, and so the book has been liberally sprinkled with photographs whose captions, hopefully, are sufficiently detailed in recording the exploits and achievements of those riders.

As well as 2022 marking the 100th anniversary of the race, it also happens to be the 75th anniversary of my first Ulster, so I count myself privileged to have seen in action most of the heroes whose names are recorded in this book.

PROGRAMME.
THE ULSTER MOTOR CYCLE CLUB.
GRAND PRIX.
140 MILES HANDICAP ROAD RACE
SATURDAY, 14th OCTOBER, 1922.
The decision of the Committee on all matters is final.
PRICE SIXPENCE.
The Ulster Motor Cycle Club, Belfast
PROGRAMME
OF THE SECOND ANNUAL
Ulster Grand Prix
Open Handicap Road Race for Motor Cycles
OVER THE ULSTER GRAND PRIX COURSE County Antrim.
DISTANCE 205 MILES,
Saturday, 15th September, 1923.
STARTING AT
LONE ENDS SCHOOL
AT TWELVE O'CLOCK.
The Ulster Motor Cycle Club, Belfast.
Official Programme
OF THE THIRD ANNUAL
ULSTER GRAND PRIX
Open Road Race for Motor Cycles,
Under Motor Cycle Union of Ireland (Ulster Centre) Rules,
6th SEPTEMBER, 1924,
Starting at CARNAUGHLIS, Co. Antrim, at 12 o'clock.
That's the Spirit! Pratts
Uniform everywhere Reliable always
PRATTS No1 Guarantee
COPYRIGHT.
ULSTER MOTOR CYCLE CLUB, BELFAST
OFFICIAL PROGRAM
OF THE FOURTH ANNUAL
ULSTER GRAND PR
OPEN ROAD RACE FOR MOTOR CYCLES
5th SEPTEMBER, 1925.
Non-Pinking — thats Prat
Uniform everywhere Reliable always
ANGLO-AMERICAN OIL CO., LTD.,
OFFICIAL PROGRAMME
THE FIFTH ANNUAL
ULSTER GRAND PRIX
OPEN ROAD RACE FOR MOTOR CYCLES
SEPTEMBER, 1926
ew T.T. Record in JUNIOR T.T. RACE won on Pratts
6d
66 MILES PER HOUR.
On top in all Road Tests
THE ULSTER MOTOR CYCLE CLUB, BELF
THE SIXTH ANNUAL
ULSTER GRAND PR
OFFICIAL PROGRAMM
& GUIDE to BEAUTY SPOT
in NORTHERN IRELAND
On SATURDAY, 3rd SEPTEMBER, 1
Starting at Carnaughlis, Co. Antrim, at 12 o'clock.
COPYRIGHT.
PRICE, SIXP
PRICE 6D.
ULSTER MOTOR CYCLE CLUB. BELFAST.
OFFICIAL
PROGRAMME
OF SEVENTH ANNUAL
Ulster Grand Prix
Incorporating
GUIDE TO ULSTER'S BEAUTY SPOTS.
Carnaughlis, - 1st September, 1928.
STARTING AT 12 NOON.
COPYRIGHT
MOTOR CYCLING
The Journal with the Green Cover
WEDNESDAYS, 3d.
Uls Grand P
7th September, 1929.
OFFICIAL PROGRA
OF EIGHTH ANNUAL
MOTOR CYCLING
For first rep of all impo events
ULSTER MOTOR CYCLE CLUB, LTD.
BELFAST
NINTH ANNUAL INTERNATIONAL
ULSTER GRAND PRIX
AT CARNAUGHLIS
6TH SEPTEMBER, 1930
Starting at 1 p.m.
1/- OFFICIAL PROGRAMME
For List of Riders see Page 34.
Copyright.
MOTOR CYCLING
The Journal with the Green Cover. Every Wednesday 3d.
will publish the
FIRST FULL REPORT OF THIS EVENT
WEDNESDAY, SEPTEMBER 10.
TENTH INTERNATIONAL
ULSTER GRAND PRIX
ULSTER MOTOR CYCLE CLUB, LTD
BELFAST
5TH SEPTEMBER 1931
Starting at 1 p.m.
OFFICIAL 1/- PROGRAMME
For List of Riders see Centre Pages
Copyright
ELEVENTH INTERNATIONAL
ULSTER GRAND PRI
ULSTER MOTOR CYCLE CLUB, LTD
BELFAST
3RD SEPTEMBER 1932
For List of Riders see Centre Pages
Copyright
For the FIRST Complete Illustrated Repo of THE ULSTER GRAND PRIX
see
MOTOR CYCLING
3D.
7th September, 1932.

CHAPTER 1

FROM HUMBLE BEGINNINGS 1922–1932

UGP trophy, 600cc class, 1923

With the political situation so unstable, Ireland in the early 1920s hardly provided the ideal setting in which to pursue the idea of launching a major sporting attraction, and yet in February 1922, at a meeting of the Irish Motor Trade in Belfast, that great Ulsterman, Harry Ferguson, moved a resolution that sought to revive interest in the business and pastime of motoring.

One of the ways that this could be done, Ferguson argued, was to promote international racing in Ireland and, fortunately, a committee of the Irish Motor Trade were persuaded by his eloquence and enthusiasm.

The first, and perhaps greatest, obstacle to Ferguson's plans, however, was the absence of legislation permitting such an event to take place. Indeed, although the Isle of Man Tourist Trophy had been established as far back as 1907, when racing resumed there in 1920 after the First World War, it was still the only motorcycle road race in the whole of the British Isles. This was primarily due to the fact that county councils elsewhere did not have the power to close public roads for the purpose of staging a race (although, it is certainly true that one or two illegal events did take place, with, or without, the connivance of the local authorities and the police – the Temple 25, held in 1921, being an outstanding example).

It is interesting that Ferguson himself selected the Clady circuit as the venue for his great race. His original intention was to stage a race for motorcycles in the morning, followed by one for cars in the afternoon. The provisional date chosen was 17 June 1922, later altered to 1 July to avoid clashing with a regatta. Ferguson and his colleagues then contacted Antrim County Council, who at once agreed to approach the newly-formed Northern Ireland government for the necessary authority to close public roads. It was at this point that the involvement of Thomas Moles MP, then editor of the *Belfast Telegraph*, proved invaluable. A keen motorcyclist himself, he more than anyone else was responsible for the Road Races Act reaching the statute book in May 1922.

Meanwhile, plans for the races proceeded, although lesser mortals could have been forgiven for throwing in the towel: not only did they have to contend with the unsettled political conditions prevailing that summer, but the committee responsible for organising the motorcar strand of the programme ultimately withdrew, which meant the motorcycle race organisers had to bear all the cost of the venture. It must have taken rare courage to proceed.

Nevertheless, on 14 October 1922, under the auspices of the Ulster Motor Cycle Club, the first Ulster Grand Prix handicap road race was held on the original 20.5 mile Clady circuit.

The race itself – which for the first two years, would start and finish at Loanends Primary School on the Seven Mile Straight (three miles before Clady Corner) – was something of a novelty at the time. The Isle of Man TT and

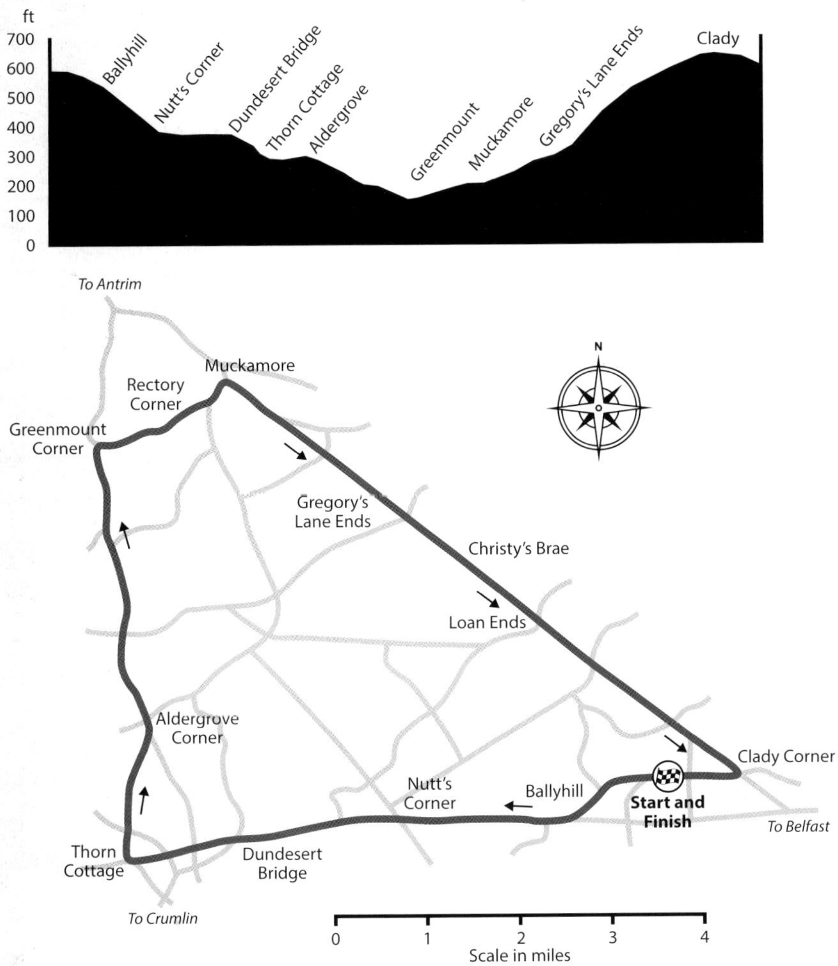

The original course at Clady, 1922–39

the continental Grands Prix were all scratch events, but the principal award at the 'Ulster', as the event would more commonly be known, was given to the winner of the race on handicap. Subsidiary prizes were offered to the fastest rider in each of four classes: 250cc, 350cc, 600cc and over 600cc. The idea of having the major award on handicap was a bold one, but it did not really catch on, and was dropped in 1924. In 1931, however, the Governor's Trophy was introduced, a prize for which every entrant was eligible to compete, on the basis of a sealed handicap. It became a much sought-after prize, but was never really considered, at least by the general public, as important as each of the class trophies.

Hubert Hassall (Norton) is escorted in after the finish, 1922. Hassall, from Birmingham, was the first winner of the Ulster Grand Prix, reaching an average speed of 60.57 mph over seven laps (143.5 miles) of the old Clady circuit – the first time a road race was won at over 60 mph.

MORTONS MEDIA GROUP LTD/MORTONS ARCHIVE

There were seventy-five entries for the first Ulster in 1922 – a remarkably good number – and all classes had to cover seven laps of the Clady circuit; a total of 143.5 miles. Thirty different makes of motorcycles were represented, including familiar names like Norton, AJS, Cotton, Harley-Davidson, BSA, Ariel, Scott and Rudge, and some that were not so well known, such as Massey-Arran, Sirrah, Mohawk, Wetherell, Pax, Ivy and Duzmo.

Several riders expressed surprise at the size of the crowds lining the circuit, with the eagerness of some spectators causing problems on the day. R.H. Wright, who officiated at the first Ulster Grand Prix as a timekeeper, reported one such problem. In that inaugural year there were no such luxuries as a scoring-board or timing-box; the timekeeping was carried out at tables placed by the roadside. After a lap or two, the spectators moved in front of the timekeepers, who then had to stand in order to see the passing riders. The spectators then sat on the tables to get a better view, whereupon the timekeepers took their chairs on to the tables, and finally ended up having to stand on the tables to see at all.

The crowd that day encroached right on to the road. As each rider approached, the throng would open up a narrow lane to let him through, and then close ranks until another appeared. Nobody seemed the slightest bit concerned about the danger.

At any rate, the entire venture was judged an unqualified success and the future of the Ulster Grand Prix was assured.

Ambition grew, and in 1924 the race became a scratch affair for four classes and the start/finish point was transferred to Carnaughlis, about a mile west of Clady Corner.

Normally the start of a race is a rather tense affair, but in 1924 the tension was relieved in spectacular fashion:

MORTONS MEDIA GROUP LTD/MORTONS ARCHIVE

Joe Craig (Norton), Clady, 1924. Born in Ballymena, Craig dominated the very early years of the Prix. In 1923, when the race was still mainly a handicap affair, he finished third overall and was fastest in the 600cc class. He won that class in 1924, when the Ulster became a scratch event, a feat he went on to repeat in 1925 and 1926. After his racing career, he became Technical Director of Norton, and his renowned engineering skill was largely responsible for enabling the single-cylinder Norton to remain competitive for so long into the era of the faster multi-cylinder racing bikes.

a bandstand had been erected behind the pit-area, over a wide, deep drain, and while the band were in the middle of the national anthem, the stand suddenly collapsed, and they plunged, somewhat untunefully, into the wreckage. The riders, already assembled on the starting grid, enjoyed a ringside view of the disaster, and when the flag fell to start the race, some of them could scarcely push their machines for laughing.

Even by 1925, the Ulster had come to be recognised as one of the important classic races, with the entry list containing no less than eight riders who had been, or were later to become, TT winners.

The following year, the capacity of the Senior class was reduced from 600cc to 500cc, and the most striking feature of the event in the late 1920s was the manner in which speeds steadily increased. In 1922, the race average of winner Hubert Hassall was 60.57 mph; however, by 1928, the 80 mph barrier had been broken (by both G.W. Walker (Rudge) at 80.08 mph and C.J.P. Dodson (Sunbeam) at 81.72 mph).

MORTONS MEDIA GROUP LTD/MORTONS ARCHIVE

The machines in the 600cc class line up for the start, 1925. The Number 52 Norton in the foreground was ridden by Joe Craig who went on to win the class. This picture gives a fair idea of what the racing scene was like in the early years of the Ulster.

An important change in the format of the race came in 1929. From 1923 to 1928, all classes had been required to cover ten laps of the course, but this had presented certain problems with regard to crowd control. In 1928, for instance, the Seniors (500cc) set off first, with the Juniors (350cc) and Lightweights (250cc) following at five-minute intervals. However, the 250cc race had taken thirty-five minutes longer to run than the 500cc class, and that, plus the ten minutes difference in starting times, meant that the leader of the 250cc class still had forty-five minutes (over two laps) to go after the 500cc winner had finished. For spectators the 500cc class was, of course, the main attraction, and it was simply impossible for the marshals and police to contain the enormous crowds for so long a time after this interest had gone. The result was that the riders in the smallest class had to complete the race on roads thronged with homegoing spectators.

From 1929 onwards, the classes were therefore graded so that each would end at approximately the same time. This meant that the Lightweights still did ten laps, but the Juniors now had to

Right: *Local rider Jimmy Shaw (Norton), complete with thick woollen socks, swings round Clady Corner on the way to finishing third in the 350cc class of the 1928 UGP. A regular competitor at the Ulster from 1922 to 1929, his proudest moment came in 1927 when he won the Senior Ulster from Frank Longman (Rudge-Whitworth) and Stanley Woods (Norton).*

W.A. MARTIN

W.A. MARTIN

MORTONS MEDIA GROUP LTD/MORTONS ARCHIVE

Stanley Woods (Norton), Clady, 1928. After failing to taste success in 1928, Stanley went on to become arguably the greatest, and certainly the most successful, rider of the pre-Second World War era. His seven victories at the Ulster Grand Prix spanned the period from 1924 to 1939 on New Imperial, Norton, and Velocette machines, and the record he set in 1939 of ten wins at the Isle of Man TT lasted for twenty-eight years before it was eclipsed by Mike Hailwood.

Leaders Ernie Nott (Rudge, 67), Graham Walker (Rudge, 80), and Stanley Woods (Norton, 63) lap a back-marker on the Seven Mile Straight during the Senior race of 1929. Walker went on to win the race, Woods finished third, while Nott crashed out. Ernie Nott competed regularly at Clady during the 1920s and 30s, and achieved several leaderboard finishes, including a win in the 250cc class in 1934. Graham Walker, who later became a well-known radio commentator, ended up with three UGP wins to his name – the Senior race in 1926 for Sunbeam, and the 1928 and 1929 Senior races for Rudge.

Stanley Woods (left) and Leo Davenport after winning the Senior and Junior classes respectively in 1930. Leo Davenport won the Junior UGP in 1929 and 1930 (on AJS), and in 1931 (on Norton) to become the first rider to win three Junior Ulsters in a row.

MORTONS MEDIA GROUP LTD/MORTONS ARCHIVE

cover eleven and the Seniors twelve. So well did the scheme work that the time difference between the winners of all three classes was less than six minutes. Indeed, in 1931, all three class winners finished within ninety seconds of each other. The problem of crowd control had, to a large extent, been solved.

After eight years of searching for the right formula, the Ulster was settling down to a recognisable pattern, but unfortunately, due to the severe economic depression of the early 1930s, the race was destined to enter perhaps the leanest years of its entire history. From 1922 to 1929, the event had attracted an average of 84 entries, but in 1930 the field was down to 65,

Stanley Woods (Norton) keeps a watchful eye on Charlie Dodson (Sunbeam) at Clady Corner in the Senior race, 1930. Woods went on to win the race by a mere eighteen seconds after more than three hours of racing. Dodson was a really interesting character, for as well as winning the 350cc Ulster in 1927, and the 250cc in 1933, he won the RAC Tourist Trophy car race on the Ards circuit in 1934. Nowadays it's difficult to imagine that someone could win a top motorcycle event and a top car racing event in consecutive years.

MORTONS MEDIA GROUP LTD/MORTONS ARCHIVE

and in 1932 entries for the three classes dropped to the lamentable total of 40. In keeping with the general mood, the racing that year was also disappointing, and to crown it all, the weather was abysmal. One wonders, in these times of sophisticated entertainment, how many people now would have the interest and patience to stand for almost three hours in the pouring rain just to witness a total of eleven riders finishing a race.

W.A. MARTIN

Top: *Front row, left to right: Sir Dawson Bates and the three class winners at the 1932 Ulster – Stanley Woods (Norton, 500cc), Ted Mellors (New Imperial, 250cc), and H.G. Tyrell-Smith (Rudge, 350cc). Mellors went on to win the Ulster on two more occasions – the 1937 and 1938 Junior races for Velocette – but the 1932 victory was H.G. Tyrell-Smith's only one at Clady.*

Bottom: *The problem of crowd control in the early days of road racing is highlighted by this shot of N. Robson (OK-Supreme) being encouraged along the Seven Mile Straight in 1932.*

MORTONS MEDIA GROUP LTD/MORTONS ARCHIVE

12TH INTERNATIONAL
ULSTER GRAND PRIX
ULSTER MOTOR CYCLE CLUB LTD
BELFAST
19TH AUGUST 1933
STARTING AT 2 P.M.
OFFICIAL
1/-
PROGRAMME
Copyright
For List of Riders see Centre Pages
For the FIRST Complete Illustrated Report of THE ULSTER GRAND PRIX
see
MOTOR CYCLING
3D.
Wednesday, 23rd August, 1933.
11TH INTERNATIONAL
ULSTER GRAND PRIX
ULSTER MOTOR CYCLE CLUB LTD
BELFAST
18TH AUGUST, 1934
STARTING AT 2 P.M.
OFFICIAL
1/-
PROGRAMME
Copyright
For List of Riders see Centre Pages
For the FIRST Complete Illustrated Report of THE ULSTER GRAND PRIX
see
MOTOR CYCLING
3D.
Wednesday, 22nd August, 1934
COPYRIGHT
For List of Riders see Centre Page
Grand Prix de l'Europe
RUN CONCURRENTLY WITH
14TH INTERNATIONAL
Ulster Grand Prix
ULSTER MOTOR CYCLE CLUB, LTD., BELFAST
24th August, 1935
OFFICIAL
1/6
PROGRAMME
Starting at 2 p.m.
For the FIRST Complete Illustrated Report of
THE ULSTER GRAND PRIX
see
MOTOR CYCLING
Bell & Logan Ltd. Belfast
COPYRIGHT
For List of Riders see Centre Page
15th CLASSIC INTERNATIONAL
Ulster Grand Prix
22nd August, 1936
Starting at 2 p.m.
OFFICIAL
1/-
PROGRAMME.
CLADY CIRCUIT
Near Belfast.
ULSTER MOTOR
CYCLE CLUB
ULSTER MOTOR CYCLE CLUB, LTD.,
98 DONEGALL PASS, BELFAST.
CORONATION YEAR
CLASSIC INTERNATIONAL
SIXTEENTH
ULSTER
GRAND PRIX
SATURDAY 21ST AUGUST 1937
OVER THE
CLADY CIRCUIT
BELFAST · N.IRELAND
OFFICIAL PROGRAMME
1/-
EACH
SEE NEXT WEDNESDAY'S ISSUE FOR THE
FIRST COMPLETE ILLUSTRATED REPORT.
MOTOR CYCLING
The Journal with the Pictorial Cover
Price 3d.
COPYRIGHT.
For List of Riders see Centre Pages.
PROMOTED BY
ULSTER MOTOR CYCLE CLUB LIMITED.
ON SAT. AUG. 20th 1938
OVER THE CLADY CIRCUIT
BELFAST - - N. IRELAND
17th
ULSTER GRAND PRIX
ROADS CLOSED 1-30 P.M.
OFFICIAL
1/6
PROGRAMME
RACES START 2-30 P.M.
MOTOR CYCLING
Edited by Graham Walker.
WEDNESDAYS—3d.
COPYRIGHT.
For List of Riders see Cent
PROMOTED BY
ULSTER MOTOR CYCLE CLUB LIMITED.
18th ULSTE
GRAND PRI
On SATURDAY, AUGUST 19th, 1939, OVER THE
CLADY CIRCUIT
BELFAST, N. IRELAND
Roads Closed 1-30 p.m.
Races Start 2-30 p.m.
Official Programme
1/-
MOTOR CYCLING
WEDNESDAYS, 3d.
DORMAN & CO., BELFAST.

CHAPTER 2

GROWING IN IMPORTANCE 1933–1942

In 1933, the tide at last turned, and the number of entries went up from 40 to 53. With a further improvement in 1934 of 64 entries, the Ulster was well and truly on the way back to being one of the best-supported events on the racing calendar.

As for the fans, they continued to amaze visitors by their tremendous enthusiasm. Even on practice days it seemed as if the entire population of Belfast was lining the roads out of the city to cheer on the competitors who, in those days, rode their machines to and from the course.

MORTONS MEDIA GROUP LTD/MORTONS ARCHIVE

Jimmy Simpson (Norton, 22) leads Jimmy Guthrie (Norton, 21) and Wal Handley (Velocette, 15) at Clady in the 1933 350cc event. These three, along with Stanley Woods, were the top riders in the 1930s. Handley won the Ulster on five occasions; Guthrie's main success came in the 1935 Ulster, which was designated as the Grand Prix d'Europe; and Simpson, who had led many races at Clady only to suffer cruel luck, finally won on his farewell appearance in 1934 by deservedly taking the 350cc trophy.

The 1934 Ulster was also memorable for quite a different reason: it was the year of the unfortunate pile-up near Ballyhill. The race had got under way in the usual manner, but as the leaders in the 500cc class approached the second left-hander, about half a mile after the start, Jimmy Guthrie (Norton) crashed into the bank and was thrown back on to the road. One after another, those following either collided into and piled on top of him, or hopped off and allowed their machines to join the pile. Amazingly, some riders got through with literally inches to spare, but even more astonishing was the fact that none of the fourteen or so riders who came off were seriously injured. One shudders at the thought of a similar incident occurring at the end of the Flying Kilo on the opening lap at today's Ulster.

Despite the significant impact the collision had on the outcome of the Senior race, the 90 mph barrier was broken for the first time that year by W.F. Rusk (Velocette) at 92.13 mph.

At this stage in road racing, there was no championship series; instead, each Grand Prix was entirely an individual affair. Each year, however, the Fédération Internationale de Motocyclisme (FIM) bestowed upon one of the classics the title of 'Grand Prix d'Europe', to indicate that it would be the most important race of the season. The Ulster Grand Prix was accorded this honour for the first time in 1935, and surely there could have been no more fitting tribute to the herculean efforts of that small band of men who only thirteen years before had defied all the odds in organising

Left: *Sharing the honours yet again were 350cc winner Wal Handley (left) and 500cc victor Jimmy Guthrie, 1935.*

W.A. MARTIN

W.A. MARTIN

Right: *Belfast's Walter Rusk receives good luck wishes from his Norton team boss Joe Craig (right) before the start of the 1935 Ulster. Known as the Blonde Bombshell, Rusk was an idol for local race fans in the 1930s. His sole win at Clady was in the 1934 Senior race when, riding a Velocette, he broke Norton's domination in the class. Perhaps his main claim to fame is that in 1939, he became the first to lap Clady at 100 mph. Sadly, Walter was killed the following year while undergoing pilot training in the RAF.*

Freddie Frith (Norton) on his way to victory as he rounds Clady Corner in front of an appreciative audience in the 1936 Senior Ulster. Frith's riding career spanned the Second World War, and his third and final UGP win in 1949 earned him the first ever 350cc World title.

MORTONS MEDIA GROUP LTD/MORTONS ARCHIVE

the first race. Saturday, 24 August 1935 was therefore to become a significant landmark in the history of the Ulster.

If the tide had turned for the event in 1933 then it reached full flood in 1935 with no fewer than seventy-nine entries – the highest number for ten years. In addition, there was, for the first time, a truly international flavour, with fifteen of the entries representing countries such as Belgium, Germany, France, Italy and Sweden. The Senior race alone contained no fewer than ten different makes of machines – Norton, DKW, Enfield, FN, New Imperial, Rudge, HHE, Velocette, Vincent HRD and Moto Guzzi – and, indeed, that year Arthur Geiss (DKW) became the first overseas rider on a non-British machine to win a class in the event.

After all the excitement and glamour surrounding 1935, one could perhaps be forgiven for expecting the following year to be something of an anti-climax, and in a sense it was. The 1936 Senior race turned out to be relatively dull

MORTONS MEDIA GROUP LTD/MORTONS ARCHIVE

The 1936 Lightweight UGP produced the closest finish of any race on either the old or the post-war Clady circuit. Ginger Wood (New Imperial, 81) was judged to be the winner over Bob Foster (New Imperial, 79), although it is difficult to tell from this picture.

with Freddie Frith (Norton) winning by an unbelievable margin of 18 min. 34 sec. – the biggest margin ever. The only excitement the day provided was in the Lightweight race which ended with Ginger Wood and Bob Foster going over the line with not more than half a wheel between the pair of them.

All in all, 1937 was a rather sad year for road racing. Jimmy Guthrie, probably the most popular rider of his era, was killed a fortnight before the Ulster – during the German Grand Prix – and his death cast a sombre atmosphere over proceedings. The weather on race day seemed to reflect the gloom, with Clady being enshrouded in thick mist and experiencing heavy rain.

On top of that the Senior class was won by a BMW machine. For those of us who have grown accustomed to the domination of Japanese-made machines in motorcycle racing, it may be difficult to appreciate the effect this victory had on all and sundry, but at that time the very thought of

Senior race winner Jock West at Ballyhill on his supercharged BMW twin, 1937. Jock repeated his victory the following year but was bitterly disappointed that, due to machine unavailability, he was forced to miss the 1939 Ulster and thus the opportunity of a hat-trick.

MORTONS MEDIA GROUP LTD/MORTONS ARCHIVE

The three class winners of the 1938 event. Left to right: Ernie Thomas (DKW, 250cc), Ted Mellors (Velocette, 350cc), and Jock West (BMW, 500cc). This was Thomas's third win at Clady, having previously won the 350cc class in 1936 and the 250cc class in 1937.

MORTONS MEDIA GROUP LTD/MORTONS ARCHIVE

MORTONS MEDIA GROUP LTD/MORTONS ARCHIVE

F.S. Cadman (Excelsior, 76) and Chris Tattersall (CTS, 71) corner at Aldergrove in the 1938 250cc race. This was an interesting part of the Clady circuit that was lost due to the wartime lengthening of the runways at the military airfield.

anything British not being best was inconceivable, and for people to have to witness such a defeat was a disaster of the greatest magnitude.

The 1938 event was unremarkable save for its poor financial outcome, which led the committee of the Ulster Motor Cycle Club (UMCC) in early 1939 to dither over whether to stage that year's race or abandon it. Only a super-optimist would have defied the gathering war clouds and risked embarking on what was an increasingly costly promotion, yet an attempt was made to obtain a grant of £200 from government sources towards the cost of promotion.

However, month after month elapsed with no sign of financial assistance and so the debate dragged on. To force the issue, an emergency meeting of the UMCC was convened at which the office

Senior race winner Dorino Serafini urges his four-cylinder Gilera to a pre-war Clady lap record of 100.03 mph in 1939. This was the Italian's one and only appearance at the Ulster. After the war, he turned his hand to car racing.

MORTONS MEDIA GROUP LTD/MORTONS ARCHIVE

bearers were faced with a decision: run the race or step aside and make room for those who would. Several ordinary members of the UMCC undertook to collect a sum that was at least equal to the non-forthcoming grant, but even that offer failed to impress those who were against taking the gamble of staging the race, and they resigned from the committee forthwith. A new committee was formed in early June, £200 was raised, and an announcement was made that the Ulster Grand Prix would be going ahead as usual.

The total number of entries received – sixty – was the smallest since 1933, but that was hardly surprising, as by August 1939, thousands were already putting on military uniforms.

The main topic of conversation on the eve of the race was whether or not the 100 mph lap would at long last be achieved, and if so who would be the first to record it. The answer wasn't long in coming for on lap three of the race, Walter Rusk, on the four-cylinder

The last meeting of international riders prior to the Second World War, August 1939. This picture was taken in Belfast during UGP week, just a fortnight before Britain declared war. From left to right: G. Hamill, J. Kirkwood, W. Forte, Siegfried Wüensche, Piero Taruffi (Gilera team manager), J. Lewis, Ernie Thomas, J.E. Little, Dorino Serafini (winner of the 1939 Senior race), Billy McMaster (secretary of the Ulster Grand Prix), and Heiner Fleischmann. In the 350cc race at the Ulster that week, German riders Fleischmann and Wüensche finished second and third respectively behind Stanley Woods.

supercharged AJS, lapped the 20.5 mile circuit in a time of 12 min. 18 sec. (exactly 100 mph).

The cheers that greeted the announcement of this feat were still echoing around the circuit when Dorino Serafini took his water-cooled supercharged Gilera 4 round in 12 min. 17.8 sec. (100.03 mph), which turned out to be the fastest lap ever recorded on the old Clady circuit. Serafini's race speed meant that the Ulster Grand Prix regained the title of the world's fastest road race; a title it had held for many years during the 1930s, but had just lost to the Swedish Grand Prix two weeks previously.

As the last of the stragglers reached the chequered flag and their machines were wheeled into the paddock on 19 August 1939, no one present could have realised that eight years would pass before the next Ulster Grand Prix at Clady. As it was, the race made a profit of 7s 6d, and two weeks later, the world was at war.

19TH CLASSIC INTERN
ULSTER GRAN
Clady Circuit
Official
ULSTER MOTOR CYCLE CLUB
GRAND PRIX of EUROP
OF THE F.I.C.M
held concurrently with the
20TH CLASSIC INTERNATIONAL
ULSTER GRAND PRIX
OVER THE CLADY CIRCUI
NORTHERN IRELAND.
AT 12 NOON.
PROMOTERS:
ULSTER MOTOR CYCLE CLUB L
Official
PROGRAM
See the
Illustrated Repor
in next Thursday's Issu
MOTOR
CYCLING
Editor:
GRAHAM WALK
ULSTER GRAND PR
CLADY CIRCUIT · 20th AUGUST.
21ST CLASSIC INTERNAT
PROMOTED BY THE ULSTER MOTOR CYCLE
OFFICIAL SOUVENIR PROGRA
BEST DESCRIPTIONS AND
PHOTOGRAPHS WILL BE IN NEXT WEEK'S
THE
MOTOR CYCL
THE WORLD'S FOREMOST MOTOR CYCLE JOURNAL.
MOTOR
CYCLING
See the
Illustrated Report in
next Thursday's issu
ULSTER
GRAND
PRIX
24th CLASSIC INTERNATIONAL
AT
CLADY CIRCUIT
Promoted by THE ULSTER MOTOR CYCLE CLUB LTD.
JUNIOR RACES 5 p.m., 14th AUGUST, 1952
SENIOR RACE 12 noon, 16th AUGUST, 1952
Roads Close on Thursday at 4 p.m. Saturday at 10.30 a.m.
OFFICIAL PROGRAMME 2/6
ULSTER MOTOR
CYCLE CLUB
PROMOTED BY THE ULSTER MOTOR CYCLE CLUB. LTD.
ULSTER GRAND PRIX
CLADY CIRCUIT
19th AUGUST 1950
22nd CLASSIC INTERNATIONAL
ROADS CLOSE AT 11 A.M
RACE STARTS 12 NOON
OFFICIAL SOUVENIR PROGRAMME 2/-
ULSTER GRAND PRIX
PROMOTED BY THE ULSTER MOTOR CYCLE CLUB LTD.
JUNIOR RACES
CLADY
CIRCUIT
SENIOR RACE
23rd CLASSIC INTERNATIONAL
OFFICIAL PROGRAMME 2/6
THE
MOTOR CYCLE
THE BEST REPORTS AND PICTURES OF ALL E
MOTOR
CYCLIN
READ WHEREVER MOTORCYCLES ARE RIDDEN
MOTOR
CYCLING
Thursdays Sixpence
FOR THE BEST REPORTS AND PICTURES

CHAPTER 3

CLADY SWANSONG 1943–1952

The Second World War wrought many changes during those dark years from 1939 to 1945; among them, changes that resulted in the post-war Clady circuit differing radically from that of the pre-war era. A new airfield constructed at Nutt's Corner led to certain alterations to the roads in the immediate area (and minimal changes to the course), but the wartime lengthening of the runways at the existing military airfield at Aldergrove was a more serious matter. This extension caused the obliteration of a stretch of circuit approximately a quarter of a mile long, and, unfortunately, the problems posed by this proved to be insurmountable.

After the war had ended, a thorough examination of the area was undertaken and it revealed that, if Aldergrove was bypassed altogether and use made of an alternative route through Killead, it would still be feasible to race over most of the old course. Offícals visited the residents of Killead, secured their goodwill, and the 'new' Clady was on the way to becoming a reality. Measuring 16.5 miles to the lap, the new circuit incorporated approximately 11 miles of the pre-war course, including the punishing Seven Mile Straight, and gave every indication that it would prove to be just as fast.

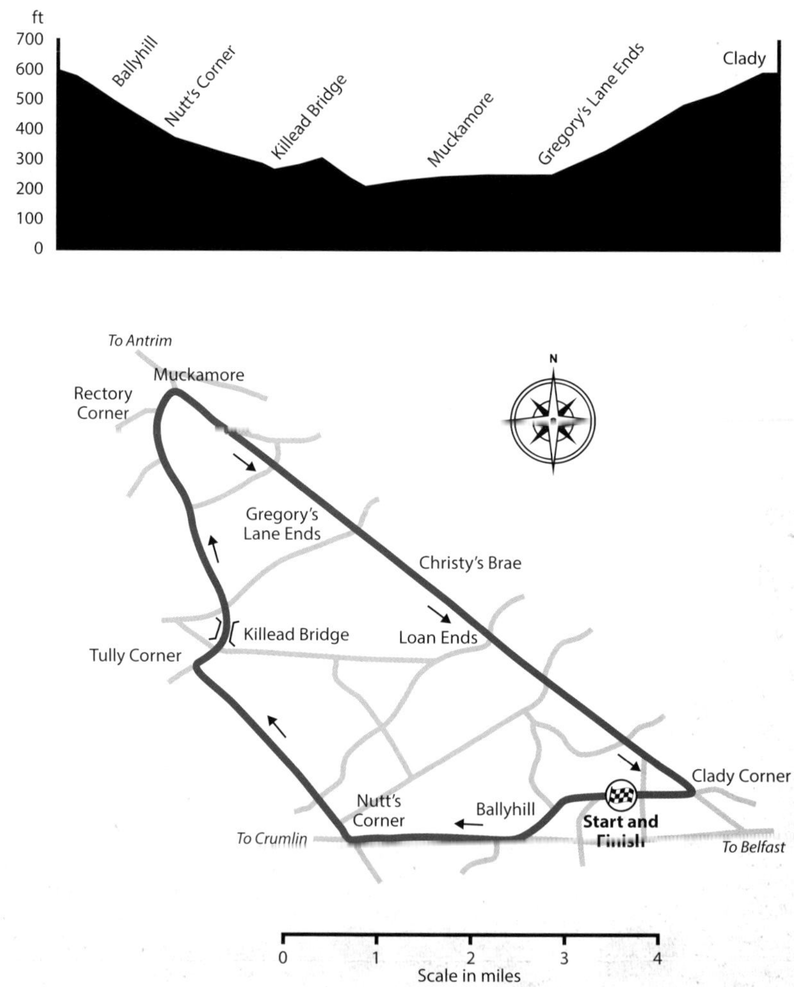

The new course at Clady, 1947–52

The older die-hards were quick to argue that, with the loss of the difficult Thorn Cottage–Aldergrove–Greenmount corner stretch plus most of the narrow section leading to Muckamore, the new circuit lacked the character of the old, and although there was some truth in this, most people felt that the course was still sufficiently arduous to ensure that it remained a real test of riding ability. Anyway, short of preventing the outbreak of the Second World War, there was no way of saving the original course.

The first event to be held over the new Clady was the Ulster Road Race on Saturday, 17 August 1946. This was not an Ulster Grand Prix, as international racing had not yet resumed, but it was a useful try-out for the 1947 Ulster. A huge crowd, eager for entertainment after the hardship and disciplines of wartime, flocked to every possible vantage point around the course that August day in 1946. Before racing commenced, those at the start/finish area witnessed a poignant ceremony in which race secretary Billy McMaster wheeled a flag-draped machine on to the grid in silent tribute to those who had sacrificed their lives during the war.

More than anything else, the 1946 event will be remembered as the year of the 'flying rubber': proper racing tyres were still not generally available, and the wartime synthetic type being used simply disintegrated at high speed. The problem naturally affected the faster and heavier machines more than the smaller ones, and only one of the thirteen starters in the 500cc class made it to the finish.

In spite of all this, the new Clady passed its test with flying colours, and the indications were that, once petrol-benzole fuel became available again it would prove to be a slightly faster circuit than the old Clady.

With the immediate post-war problem of tyre and engine reliability having been ironed out, the organisers boldly decided to increase the race distances for the 1947 Ulster to slightly beyond even the mileages covered pre-war. Fifty-nine entries had been received, which was understandable considering the dearth of race-worthy machines and the fact that quite a few riders were still in the services.

The weather rose to the occasion and the circuit was bathed in glorious sunshine, but unfortunately for spectators, an industrial dispute had halted bus services over the weekend and, as five hundred buses had been required to convey racegoers to Clady for the 1946 Ulster Road Race, this posed a serious problem. Thousands of fans coped by boarding Belfast Corporation trams that ran to Ligoniel

MORTONS MEDIA GROUP LTD/MORTONS ARCHIVE

Artie Bell (Norton, 1) and Les Graham (AJS, 17) battle it out in the 1948 Senior Ulster, which carried, for the second time, the title of Grand Prix d'Europe. Bell was forced to retire while disputing the lead with the eventual winner, Enrico Lorenzetti, and Graham finished third. Conditions were so poor that day – with torrential rain and a howling gale – that it proved impossible to write a single figure on the giant scoreboard, which was in danger of being blown down.

on the northern outskirts of the city, and then walking the considerable distance to Clady Corner. Others travelled by seven special trains to Muckamore, the nearest railway station to the circuit, but this meant that the crowds at Clady Corner and Muckamore were far in excess of normal. Consequently, the start of the race had to be delayed while marshals dealt with the situation and the organisers were satisfied that the roads were clear.

The next year, for the second time in its illustrious history, the Ulster Grand Prix was accorded the honour of being selected as the Grand Prix d'Europe, but I would venture to suggest that anyone who was there for race day on 21 August 1948 may well remember the occasion for quite a different reason – the weather.

It was one of those days that started badly … and steadily grew worse. In the early morning it was drizzling; by 11 a.m. it was raining heavily; and by the start of the race it was blowing almost a hurricane. It was the sort of rainstorm that normally wears itself out within a few minutes, but at Clady that day it continued for hours and lasted the entire duration of the race. At one point, it was feared that the giant scoreboard might be blown down, and although this did not happen, the posting of times and leaderboard positions had to be abandoned.

It was a day of absolute misery for officials and spectators, but it must have been sheer agony for the riders. Small wonder that of the 93 courageous starters, only 28 completed the course. So ended the 1948 Grand Prix d'Europe. The Ulster may have lost the title of world's fastest road race, but it gained a new one – the world's wettest.

The year 1949 heralded yet another milestone in the story of the Ulster: the Grand Prix Road-Racing World Championship was born, and the Ulster Grand Prix was selected as one of its six races. As it was the penultimate race in the series, the championship had reached an intriguing stage by the time of the Ulster, and when Les Graham won the Senior class at Clady, he became the first ever 500cc World Champion.

The following year, Norton successfully pioneered a revolutionary motorcycle design which became known as the 'Featherbed'. The brainchild of Rex McCandless, it kept at bay the threat of multi-cylinder machines a little longer than would otherwise have been the case. This development coincided with the arrival in the Norton team of Geoff Duke, a winning combination from the start. In the process of stamping his authority on the Senior Ulster of 1950, Duke eclipsed Serafini's 1939 lap record with a speed of 101.77 mph.

When in 1951 the FIM introduced a rule that all competitors in world

FOTTOFINDERS

MORTONS MEDIA GROUP LTD/MORTONS ARCHIVE

Top: *Nello Pagani astride his 500cc Gilera on the starting grid at the 1949 race. On this his first visit to Clady, Pagani surprised a lot of people by finishing in a well-deserved third place. In contrast to the previous year, racing took place in glorious sunshine.*

Bottom: *Les Graham swings his AJS Porcupine twin round Tully Corner on his way to victory in the 1949 Senior race. This was the year of the first FIM World Championship and the Ulster Grand Prix was selected as one of its six events. Graham went on to be crowned the first ever 500cc World Champion.*

Bottom: *Geoff Duke rounds Clady Corner on his way to victory, 1950. Duke burst on to the racing scene that year with his newly developed Featherbed Norton, smashing race and lap records to smithereens.*

Right: *Arthur 'Artie' James Bell at the 1949 Ulster. Winner of the 1947 Senior Ulster, the 1948 Senior Isle of Man TT, and the 1950 Junior TT, Artie was idolised by local race fans in the immediate post-war era. He was involved in an accident while competing in the 1950 Belgian Grand Prix and sustained injuries that ended his racing career.*

MORTONS MEDIA GROUP LTD/MORTONS ARCHIVE

FOTTOFINDERS

Umberto Masetti at Muckamore, about to tackle the Seven Mile Straight, 1950. The Italian rider was one of the favourites for the 500cc race, but somehow never got to grips with the bumpy nature of the circuit, and ended up a disappointing sixth. Despite his Ulster setback, he went on to become World Champion that year.

FOTTOFINDERS

The four class winners on the rostrum at Clady, 1950. From left to right: Geoff Duke (500cc), Bob Foster (350cc), Maurice Cann (250cc) and Carlo Ubbiali (125cc). Foster became 350cc World Champion in 1950; Cann had just won his fourth Lightweight UGP in a row; and Ubbiali went on to become World Champion nine times.

FOTTOFINDERS

Accomplished Italian rider Bruno Ruffo at Tully Corner, on his way to winning the Lightweight Ulster, 1951. That year, on his Moto Guzzi, Ruffo regained the 250cc World Championship title he had first won two years previously.

championship road races must be given the opportunity to ride in more than one class at each meeting, the organisers of the Ulster were faced with a choice: the Continental solution of running shorter races or hold a more ambitious two-day event that would enable the races to be run over the traditional full distance. Thankfully they chose the latter option and succeeded in coping admirably with the additional necessary arrangements.

Alas, the 1951 event was to be overshadowed by the awful tragedy that occurred on the Wednesday of race week. Three members of the Moto Guzzi works team – Enrico Lorenzetti, Gianni Leoni and Sante Geminiani – were touring on open roads in close company to improve their knowledge of the circuit. All three of them rounded Clady Corner, but on reaching the pit area, Geminiani and Lorenzetti slowed to a halt. Leoni continued on, but by Ballyhill had realised his teammates' absence and decided to return to the pits. Meanwhile, Lorenzetti and Geminiani had set off again in pursuit of their colleague, and on the long bend between the Grandstand and Ballyhill, Leoni and Geminiani collided head-on. Leoni was killed almost instantly, and Geminiani died soon afterwards in the Royal Victoria Hospital in Belfast.

Most people were unaware of it at the time, but 16 August 1952 would become a significant date in the history of the Ulster Grand Prix; the date on which racing took place for the last time over the world-famous Clady circuit. The 1951 experiment of staging the event over two days had been repeated, and indeed was to become a regular feature for several years. Not so popular, though, was the new arrangement of having one of the official practice periods scheduled from 5 a.m. to 7 a.m. on the Wednesday.

Those competitors anxious to make the most of the practice time available were to discover that at 5 a.m., night still lay black over the Antrim countryside. Some of the riders did not find such an early start the least bit amusing.

Despite only being offered a chance to ride a works Gilera on the eve of the race, and thus having little time to familiarise himself with the bike, local favourite Cromie McCandless became the last rider to win the Ulster at Clady, and Les Graham on the MV Agusta became the fastest rider to ever lap either of the Clady circuits with a time of 9 min. 21 sec. (105.94 mph).

Surely there could not have been a more dramatic and wonderful climax to beloved Clady; a race truly worthy of the occasion. Perhaps it was just as well, though, that most people present did not realise they were witnessing Clady's swansong, for, armed with such dreadful knowledge, how sad it would have been to reflect that places like Ballyhill, Tully Corner, Killead Bridge, Muckamore, the Seven Mile Straight, and dear old Clady Corner itself would never again echo to the sound of racing engines.

MORTONS MEDIA GROUP LTD/MORTONS ARCHIVE

FOTTOFINDERS

Top: *Les Graham (MV, 11), Reg Armstrong (Norton, 1) and Ken Kavanagh (Norton, 4) battle it out in the Senior race around Ballyhill, 1952. Unfortunately, due to various problems, all three were forced out of the race – which turned out to be one of the most exciting ever witnessed at Clady – but not before Graham recorded the fastest ever Clady lap at 105.94 mph. This was the last year the Ulster would be held on that classic circuit.*

Bottom: *Local rider Cromie McCandless passes Killead Church in the 500cc race, 1952. Gilera team manager Piero Taruffi had created something of a sensation on the eve of the race by offering McCandless the injured Alfredo Milani's works bike. At various stages, the race produced four different leaders: Ken Kavanagh (Norton), Les Graham (MV), Reg Armstrong (Norton) and Jack Brett (AJS). McCandless held a lowly ninth place on the first lap, but due to all of the above experiencing problems, he inherited the lead on the final lap and holds the honour of winning the last race held at Clady.*

25TH CLASSIC INTERNATIONAL
LSTER GRAND PRIX
UNDROD CIRCUIT
AUGUST 13TH & 15TH 1953
OFFICIAL PROGRAMME 2/6
ULSTER GRAND PRIX
DUNDROD CIRCUIT
JUNE 24th & 26th, 1954
OFFICIAL PROGRAMME 2/6
MOTOR CYCLING
READ WHEREVER MOTORCYCLES ARE RIDDEN
THURSDAYS EIGHTPENCE
27th CLASSIC INTERNATION
Ulster
GRAND PRIX
MOTOR CYCLE CLUB
AUG
11th & 13th,
DUNDROD CIRC
NORTHERN IR
THE
MOTOR CY
will bring it home to you.
OFFICIAL PROGRAMME 2/6
28th CLASSIC INTERNATIONAL
Ulster
Grand Prix
AUGUST 9th-11th 1956
DUNDROD CIRCUIT
NORTHERN IRELAND
OFFICIAL PROGRAMME 2/6
29th CLASSIC INTERNATIONAL
ULSTER
GRAND PRIX
DUNDROD CIRCUIT
NORTHERN IRELAND
10 AUGUST
1957
The Journal with all the News and Pictures
MOTOR CYCLING
CLASSIC 30th INTERNATIONAL
ULSTER
GRAND
PRIX
DUNDROD
CIRCUIT
2/6
Official Programme
THE
MOTOR CYCLE
THURSDAYS
OFFICIAL PROGRAMME 2s.
31st CLASSIC INTERNATIONAL
ULSTER GRAND PRIX
Dundrod Circuit, Northern Irelan
8 August 1959
OFFICIAL PROGRAMME 2s 6d
33rd
CLASSIC INTERNATIONAL
ULSTER
GRAND PRIX
DUNDROD CIRCUIT
NORTHERN IRELAND
12 AUGUST 1961
IAL PROGRAMME 2s. 6d.
CLASSIC INTERNATIONAL
STER GRAND PRIX
Dundrod Circuit, Northern Ireland
6th August 1960
MOTOR CYCLING
COOTER WEEKLY
Official Programme
CLASSIC INTERNATIONAL
34th ulster grand p
DUNDROD CIRCUIT
NORTHERN IRELAND
AUGUST 11,

DONNELLAN PHOTOGRAPHIC ARCHIVES

Ireland's Corner, 1954. Anyone familiar with the Dundrod circuit will know how different this stretch looks today. It is horrifying to think what would happen if the trees were still present and an accident occurred, given the difference in speeds since 1954. Guy Martin's crash at that spot in 2015 springs to mind.

added to the two-day programme. Although Dundrod initially lacked the atmosphere and traditions associated with Clady, apprehension over the future of the event proved groundless for the new course was an unqualified success with the riders, and even most of the die-hards grudgingly admitted that Dundrod wasn't that bad after all.

A somewhat startling break with tradition came in 1954 when the Ulster was held in the month of June. This had come about in response to suggestions that it would be advantageous to stage the event immediately after the Isle of Man TT races, thus saving international competitors the expense of a second trip later in the year. It was also argued that, weatherwise, June was preferable to August. But with prolonged and heavy showers on both days, plus the absence of Moto Guzzi and MV Agusta due to a combination of machine mortality at the TT and the failure to negotiate agreeable terms with the organisers of the UGP, spectator attendance was sparse.

Another innovation in 1954 was the running of all five classes separately, although the decision to hold the 500cc race on the Thursday instead of on the Saturday was severely criticised by the public and turned out to be extremely unpopular. By the end of the meeting, the organisers were completely fed up, but resolute in one thing – never again to stage the Prix in June.

In 1955, the 125cc Ultra-Lightweight

MORTONS MEDIA GROUP LTD/MORTONS ARCHIVE

In what was his Ulster Grand Prix debut, Belfast's Sammy Miller sweeps his 250cc NSU Sportmax through Leathemstown to second place in 1955. Sammy became more famous as a Trials rider, winning the British title on eleven occasions, and was European Trials Champion twice.

and Sidecar races were axed and the meeting consisted of only three classes – 500cc, 350cc and 250cc. Nevertheless, perhaps because of the fine weather or the host of new records that were established, the Ulster that year was one of the most successful and enjoyable for a long time, despite the competition from the Great Britain vs Rest of Europe soccer match taking place in Belfast's Windsor Park on 13 August.

The UMCC had more than their share of unexpected problems over the years, but the one they were saddled with in 1956 must have taxed even their resources to the limit. For three years the Ulster Grand Prix had shared Dundrod with two major car races – the RAC Tourist Trophy and the Ulster Trophy – but after the tragic accident in the 1955 Le Mans 24-hour race in which over eighty spectators were killed, there was a dark cloud over motor racing. A few months later, a series of fatal accidents in the RAC Tourist Trophy itself finally put paid to any idea of Dundrod's suitability for car racing. The RAC cancelled the 1956 TT, and in doing so, unintentionally struck the Ulster a heavy blow as the organisers were left with the formidable burden of shouldering the total cost of race promotion on the Dundrod circuit. Despite this serious setback, however, they went ahead with the 1956 event, and indeed, reverted to the 1954 format by reintroducing the 125cc and Sidecar classes to the programme.

After the dust had settled on the 1956 event, a great deal of heart-searching went on behind the scenes before details of the 1957 meeting were released. For a variety of reasons, including the need to reduce promotional costs, the decision was taken to revert to a one-day meeting. This of course meant finding time from somewhere, so the programme was pruned by shortening the races and abolishing the Sidecar class altogether. Many regretted this move,

Top: *Libero Liberati (Gilera) exits the Hairpin in 1957. It was something of a surprise that Italian rider Liberati upstaged his two Gilera teammates – Geoff Duke and Bob McIntyre – on a circuit more suited to their skills than his own. He did, though, and his convincing victory also saw him become 500cc World Champion.*

Bottom: *Bob McIntyre (Gilera), just after the Hairpin during the 500cc race, 1957. Two months before that year's Ulster, McIntyre became the first to lap the Isle of Man TT mountain course at 100 mph, but he had to wait until 1961 for his only UGP win (250cc class).*

MORTONS MEDIA GROUP LTD/MORTONS ARCHIVE

for undoubtedly the Sidecar races had added colour and spectacle to the scene, while the purists argued that a Senior Ulster of a mere 150 miles was no race at all. Nevertheless, the meeting was voted a tremendous success, and a new pattern for the future had been set.

When the 1958 season got under way, the whole racing scene was virtually unrecognisable from that of twelve months previously. In the first place, the FIM had banned the use of full streamlining. meaning that fairings would only be permitted as long as they did not enclose the rider or the front wheel. At the same time came the far

MV teammates John Hartle (left) and John Surtees arrive in Belfast for the 1959 Ulster. Come race day they ended up at opposite ends of the success spectrum. Surtees easily won both 350cc and 500cc races, while Hartle needed medical attention after clouting the bank at Tornagrough in the 350cc event, and missed the 500cc race as a result. Surtees ended his motorcycling career with six Ulster wins, and Hartle with two.

more startling news that Gilera, Moto Guzzi and Mondial were withdrawing from racing, thus following the trend started by factories such as Norton, AJS, NSU and DKW. The effect on the sport was devastating, and even though MV Agusta decided to continue its support, there was no doubt that the golden age of racing was at an end.

With MV beginning to dominate the international road racing scene, one would have been justified in predicting a dull and uninteresting 1959 Ulster, but with their decision not to contest the 125cc and 250cc classes at Dundrod, this was one occasion when their absence actually enhanced the racing and led to a greater uncertainty about the outcome. It also, incidentally, resulted in Mike Hailwood (125cc Ducati) securing his first ever World Championship victory.

In 1960, all race and lap records at Dundrod were broken. It was also the year in which the invasion of Japanese motors first hit the Ulster, though the two things were unrelated. Honda, the pioneer in those days, may have

Alberto Gandossi (MZ, 2), Carlo Ubbiali (MV, 8) and Gary Hocking (MV, 9) exit Leathemstown during the 125cc race, 1960. This race turned out to be a nail-biting affair as these three riders were never more than yards apart. Even after Gandossi crashed out just after half distance, Ubbiali and Hocking continued the scrap, with the former getting the verdict by one-fifth of a second. In his short career, Hocking ended up with three UGP wins.

MORTONS MEDIA GROUP LTD/MORTONS ARCHIVE

contested the Isle of Man TT a year earlier, but they were no match for the works MVs.

It was quite a different story in 1961, though, with Honda filling the entire podium in the 250cc Ulster – Bob McIntyre, Mike Hailwood and Jim Redman came first, second and third respectively – and also winning the 125cc class with Kunimitsu Takahashi.

In 1962, they went one better by winning three of the four classes contested: 350cc with Jim Redman; 250cc with Tommy Robb; and 125cc with Luigi Taveri. That year, however, fans had gathered at Dundrod with heavy hearts, for news had just filtered through that Bob McIntyre, one of the most popular riders ever to have raced at the Ulster, lay critically ill after crashing at Oulton Park. He died only a few days after the Prix.

Ten years had passed since the demise of Clady, and there could now be absolutely no doubt whatsoever that Dundrod had been an outstanding success – and had proved the critics wrong.

OFFICIAL PROGRAMME 2s. 6d.
35th Classic International
ULSTER GRAND PRIX
DUNDROD CIRCUIT, NORTHERN IRELAND
10 August 1963
HONDA
72
CLASSIC INTERNATIONAL
36th
ULSTER
GRAND
PRIX
DUNDROD CIRCUIT
NORTHERN IRELAND
Motor
Cycling
37th. CLASSIC
INTERNATIONAL
ULSTER
GRAND
PRIX
DUNDROD CIRCUIT
NORTHERN IRELAND
HELD UNDER F.I.M. RULES
AUGUST 7th. 1965
OFFICIAL PROGRAM
SPONSORED BY
Gallaher Ltd.
OFFICIAL PROGRAMME 2/6
39th CLASSIC INTERNATIONAL
ULSTER GRAND PRIX
DUNDROD CIRCUIT
40th Classic International
ULSTER
GRAND
PRIX
22
DUNDROD CIRCUIT
AUGUST 17th 1968.
held under F.I.M. rules
th CLASSIC INTERNATIONAL
Jlster Grand Prix
undrod Circuit, Belfast
ugust 20th 1966
Gallaher sponsored promotion!
42nd Classic International
Ulster Grand Prix
DUNDROD
15th Aug. 1970
NIETO
ENDERS
SIMMONDS
41st Classic International
ULSTER
GRAND PRIX
NDROD
16th Aug. 1969.
OFFICIAL
SOUVENIR
PROGRAMME
3/-
43RD CLASSIC INTERNATIONA
ULSTER GRAND PRI
14th August 1971
DUNDR

CHAPTER 6

A DECADE OF DESPAIR 1973–1982

Little did anyone realise, in 1971, the dark days that lay ahead for the Ulster. In October 1971 a terrorist bomb caused substantial damage to Grand Prix House. Then in 1972 came the tragic and untimely death of Bertie Mann, chair of Ulster Centre Promotions and a man who, over many years, had contributed much to the event.

BERTIE MARTIN

John Williams after his treble win – 500cc, 350cc, and 250cc – at Dundrod in 1973, when he became the first rider to win three UGP races in one day. Williams, from Cheshire, was a six-time winner at the Ulster and was one of the most popular riders of the 1970s. A trophy in his honour is still awarded in the Isle of Man to the rider who records the fastest lap in the TT Superbike race.

Public support for the Supporters' Club had slumped to its lowest ebb since 1964, and in 1972, amid Northern Ireland's worsening political and social situation – including the dissolution of the parliament at Stormont – promoters were forced to cancel that year's race. In its place, a substitute 'national' event was held at Bishopscourt airfield.

In the midst of all the gloom and despair, however, was at least one cause for optimism: before its dissolution, the Northern Ireland parliament had enacted legislation permitting the race promoters to levy a charge on spectators entering the Dundrod area. Up to 1971, a charge had been imposed on vehicles, but many spectators were still able to enjoy a full day's entertainment at virtually no cost. Now that this loophole had at last been plugged, it was hoped there would be a beneficial effect on the revenue from future races.

With the future uncertain, the FIM decided not to grant championship status to the Ulster for 1973, although they did issue an international permit for the event, which comprised the same four classes as in 1971 – 500cc, 350cc, 250cc and Sidecar. John Williams emerged as the 'Man of the Meeting' by winning all three solo races, thus becoming the first man ever to win three classes in one day at the Ulster.

For a pleasant change, the 1974 Ulster was free from controversy, although mindful of the continuing uncertainty regarding the political situation, the organisers had decided not to press the FIM for world championship status. By this time it was looking increasingly unlikely that such status would ever return as, following the unfortunate death of Gilberto Parlotti in the 1972 Isle of Man TT, the campaign to remove all pure road circuits from the championship had gathered momentum. In fact, in 1974, some of the top riders had already taken matters into their own hands by

CHAPTER 7

TT F1 & JOEY TO THE RESCUE 1983–1992

After all the negative publicity in the wake of the 1982 event, Ulster Centre Promotions responded by negotiating a five-figure sponsorship deal with Prentice Ltd, a locally based car dealership. This was something of a coup considering that the UK was right in the middle of an economic recession, and the infusion of cash was much needed. The FIM were now enforcing increased amounts for world championship prizemoney (a minimum level had been set), so a major slice of the Ulster's budget had to go to the TT Formula 1 race.

ROWLAND WHITE

ROWLAND WHITE

Top: *Mick Grant (Honda) in the 1980 TT F1 race in which he finished third. Although he was destined never to taste success at the Ulster Grand Prix, the Yorkshireman was, nevertheless, a formidable opponent. He was runner-up in UGP races on four occasions, including twice in the prestigious TT F1 events of 1983 and 1985.*

Bottom: *Norman Brown (Suzuki) leads Ron Haslam (Honda) and Mick Grant (Suzuki) out of Leathemstown and up the hill to Tullyrusk, 1982, in a shot that typifies the closely fought battles in the TT F1 races of the early 1980s.*

As a result, the organisers were forced to trim the 1983 race programme, and the class to suffer was the 1000cc Superbikes. The five races making up the meeting that year were therefore TT F2, 350cc, TT F1, 250cc and 500cc, in that order.

In June 1984, the race organisers were dealt a crippling blow when Prentice suddenly withdrew their sponsorship (the UCP had been led to understand that their involvement would be for a minimum of two years). Nevertheless, the organisers succeeded, at very short notice, in enlisting the financial assistance of three local companies, including overall sponsor Jim Finlay of the food processing firm JAS Finlay, who agreed also to sponsor the main TT Formula 1 race. The overall budget for the meeting was £70,000 (including £40,000 prize money) and the Supporters' Club promised a welcome contribution of £22,000.

This was also the year in which rumours circulated of a rift between Joey Dunlop and the Honda camp over the perceived feeling that Honda would prefer Joey's teammate, Roger Marshall, to win the world title. Although this was strenuously denied, things came to the boil at Dundrod when Joey passed Marshall at the Windmill on the last lap to win the race – that year Joey won not

ROWLAND WHITE

Phil Mellor (Yamaha) in the 1982 350cc race where he was pipped to the win by Ray McCullough. Mellor, another Yorkshireman, was a great supporter of Irish road racing, including the national events. He had three wins at the UGP, including the first ever Superstock race in 1986, and was runner-up to Tony Rutter in the 1983 TT Formula 2 World Championship.

New Zealander Dennis Ireland signs autographs in the Dundrod paddock, 1983. His best result at the Ulster Grand Prix was third place in the 1985 500cc race. The two children on the right of the photograph are my son and daughter.

Joey Dunlop (right) and Brian Reid at a function celebrating their respective wins of the 1985 TT F1 and TT F2 World Championships. That year, Northern Ireland had two motorcycling world title holders.

only the F1 TT, but the 500cc and 250cc races as well – and a furious Marshall threatened to lodge a protest on the grounds that the pass was dangerous.

In 1985, Joey continued his domination of the sport with yet another hat-trick at the Ulster. He again won the 250cc and 500cc races and secured his fourth TT F1 title in a row. Alas, 1985 would be the last occasion on which the historic 500cc class was held at the Prix, ending an unbroken run which had begun in 1926. That year he was joined by Brian Reid (Yamaha) whose win at Dundrod gave him the TT F2 championship.

In February 1986, Ulster Centre Promotions secured a major sponsor

EDDIE MATEER

Brian Reid in the warm-up paddock at Dundrod, 1990, prior to the last ever TT F1 race held at the Ulster. Reid was TT F2 World Champion in 1985 and 1986, had five wins at the Isle of Man TT, nine at the Ulster Grand Prix from 1982 to 1992, and won numerous national events in Ireland. In 1982, he became the first person to win three Irish road racing championships in the same year: 500cc, 350cc and 250cc. Reid's motorcycling career was cut short in 1994 when he suffered injuries in a racing accident.

in the Shell Oil Company and announced that the event would be called the Shell Ulster Grand Prix. Shell had undertaken to sponsor the TT F1 World Championship round at Dundrod as well as the Senior race, which for 1986 was for machines up to 1000cc. Also added to the programme for the first time was a race for Superstock machines.

That year, Joey managed to wrap up his fifth TT F1 title in succession, while Brian Reid repeated his TT F2 championship success. Reid would be the last ever TT F2 champion, as the class ended in 1986 (the short-lived TT F3 class had been terminated much earlier in 1981).

The 1987 Ulster Grand Prix was one that generated more debate and news coverage than had been the case for a long time, but, unfortunately, for the wrong reasons. The year had begun well – speculation about the imminent disbanding of TT F1 had been proved groundless, plus the end of June brought the exciting development that the Ulster was to be sponsored by BBC Radio Ulster – but the event itself ended in tragedy.

Wednesday's practice session took place in very wet conditions and, as a result, TT F1 championship leader, Virginio Ferrari (Yamaha), called the Dundrod circuit dangerous, and pulled out of the meeting. It was cloudy but dry

DEREK McINTYRE

Steven Cull leads Joey Dunlop into Tornagrough in the 1985 Ulster. Cull was one of our top racing stars of the 1980s. His first road race win was at the Temple 100 in 1975, and he recorded two Isle of Man TT victories and three wins at the Ulster Grand Prix. Cull was forced to retire from racing in 1991 following a serious accident at Oliver's Mount, Scarborough.

when race day began that Saturday, but by the time the TT F1 machines were on their warm-up lap, it had started to rain heavily. The start was delayed while riders took the opportunity to change tyres, but unfortunately the weather got even worse. The clerk of the course sensibly delayed the start for one hour in the hope that things would improve, but decided eventually to go ahead, even though a few of the riders had expressed their concern at the prospect of racing.

In blinding spray, the field got away, some riders actually jumping the start because, it was alleged, they couldn't see the green light properly. Then, at the end of the opening lap, at the right-hand kink after the pit-area, Klaus Klein (Yamaha) appeared to aquaplane and crashed heavily into the bank. He was killed instantly. The race was stopped, the mood sombre, and with the rain continuing to pour down, the remainder of the meeting was abandoned.

For weeks afterwards, recriminations

were rife, with many people expressing the view that the race should never have been started; although, ironically, Klein was one rider who had been keen to get the race going.

Naturally, in view of what had happened in 1987, the promoters had a real task on their hands to come up with a good entry in 1988, and it was no surprise that all their best efforts met with very little success. Indeed, gloomy forecasts circulated that the very future of the Ulster was in jeopardy unless the organisers could come up with some radical changes to the format. Sure, the TT F1 class had, in some ways, been a lifeline for the Ulster, but one wonders whether even that would have been sufficient if Joey Dunlop hadn't been around at the same time.

In the end, the programme for 1988 consisted of the TT F1 class, Superbike, Superstock and two separate 350cc races, and the prize fund was boosted by the UGP Supporters' Club, who donated a staggering £25,000 in celebration of the club's 25th anniversary.

For 1989, Ulster Centre Promotions certainly came up with new ideas. Not all of them were warmly welcomed, but at least an attempt was being made to bring the Prix into line with the evolving racing classes. The TT F1 was to be backed up by five other races – 600cc and 400cc Supersport (two new classes),

DONNELLAN PHOTOGRAPHIC ARCHIVES

Eddie Laycock chats in the Dundrod paddock, 1988. Laycock was the most successful rider from the Republic of Ireland since Reg Armstrong. He finished runner-up to Brian Reid in the 1986 TT Formula 2 World Championship, and between 1986 and 1989, his successes included two Isle of Man TT victories and five wins at the Ulster. From 1988 to 1992, Eddie concentrated on the 500cc Grand Prix World Championship before retiring.

JOHN TENNANT

Carl Fogarty on his Honda in 1988, the year he first competed at the Ulster Grand Prix. He won the TT Formula 1 race that year, the first of three TT Formula 1 World Championship titles. Renowned for his aggressive competitiveness, Fogarty would later rewrite the record books in the World Superbike series by winning a total of fifty-nine races on his way to amassing no less than four World Superbike titles.

Superbikes, 350cc and, for the first time in eleven years, a Sidecar race. UCP had also managed to secure Guinness as their overall event sponsor, and at the end of the meeting, most observers agreed that things had definitely improved on the previous year.

For the 1990 Ulster, the six-race format was reduced to five, with the axing of the 400cc Supersport and Sidecar events, and the inclusion of the 125cc class for the first time since 1968. The bad news for the Prix was that, although the TT F1 race was still on the programme, it was officially no longer a world championship event – the series had been given instead the title of World Coupe at the 1989 FIM Autumn Congress.

Guinness were the main sponsors of the Prix for a second year in 1990, although their late request not to have their brand name appear on the front cover of the race programme caused consternation as the programme had to be reprinted and was not available until the eve of practice. Most fans went home happy after the meeting, however, having witnessed exciting racing in which the podium finishers for both the 600cc and 125cc races were separated by a mere second.

As expected, in October 1990, the FIM finally decided to end the TT F1 World Championship series, even though seven different countries had expressed an interest in hosting a round. This news obviously had serious consequences for the future of the Ulster, although the promoters tried to put a brave face on it, saying that the class had been too expensive to run anyway. On top of this, Guinness, pulled their sponsorship of the 1991 event, though this too had been expected.

All of this was, however, overshadowed by a controversy that had simmered all winter and spring of 1990/91 over a proposal to introduce a chicane at the start and finish areas of the UGP. Plans also included the erection of permanent pit facilities on the opposite side of the road than they were at present. The plans were passed by the Ulster Centre Roads Inspection Committee, but riders were divided on the safety aspect. In any event, no changes were to be made before the 1991 race, so things settled down again.

The programme had been tweaked yet again for 1991 – with two Superbike races, two 350cc races, plus one each of 600cc, 400cc and 125cc – and the meeting was mostly memorable for the fact that Phillip McCallen (Honda) won his first ever Ulster.

The dreaded chicane was finally ready for the 1992 meeting and, as some riders had predicted, it did pose a potentially dangerous situation on the exit. Some modifications were made for the final practice session, and race day, held that year on 20 June, passed off incident-free as far as the chicane was concerned.

The only highlight of note in an otherwise low-key meeting was Robert Dunlop's Superbike win on a Norton; their first UGP success for twenty-seven years.

CLIFFORD McLEAN/PACEMAKER PRESS INTERNATIONAL

Steve Hislop (Honda) on his way to victory in the TT Formula 1 race in the 1989 Ulster. Hislop's first time at Dundrod was in 1986, and he tasted victory twice at the Ulster. In 1989, he became the first rider to lap the Isle of Man TT course at over 120 mph, and although he won eleven races at the TT, and was British Superbike Champion twice, it is perhaps true to say that he never fully realised his potential.

SIXTY-FOURTH INTERNATIONAL
ULSTER GRAND PRIX
sponsored by
PEPSI
Dundrod circuit
7 August 1993
ULSTER GRAND PRIX
sponsored by
CP Hire Ltd
Foremost in Plant Hire
Dundrod Circuit, Lisburn, Co. Antrim
Saturday 19th August 2000
Race Area Admission and Programme £12.00
Promoted by
Coleraine & District Motor Club
ULSTER
GRAND PRI
Coleraine
Ballymena
Belfast
Plant Hire Ltd.
Foremost in Plant Hire
SATURDAY 19TH AUGUST 19
Venue
DUNDROD • LISBURN • CO. ANT
Promoter:
COLERAINE & DISTRICT MOTOR CLUB LTD.
OFFICIAL SOUVENIR PROGRAMME £5.0
SIXTY-SEVENTH INTERNATIONAL
ULSTER GRAND PRIX
In Association With
Telegraph
Promoter:
COLERAINE & DISTRICT MOTOR CLUB LTD.
SATURDAY 3RD AUGUST 1996
Venue - DUNDROD • LISBURN • CO. ANTRIM
SIXTY-EIGHTH INTERNATIONAL
ULSTER GRAND PRIX
Coleraine
Ballymena
Belfast
Plant Hire Ltd.
Foremost in Plant Hire
In Association With
Belfast Telegraph
The National Newspaper of Northern Ireland
Promoter:
COLERAINE & DISTRICT MOTOR CLUB LTD.
SATURDAY 23RD AUGUST 1997
Venue - DUNDROD • LISBURN • CO. ANTRIM
SEVENTIETH INTERNATIONA
ULSTER
GRAND PRI
Dundrod Circuit, Lisburn, Co Antr
Saturday 21st August 1999
Promoted by
Coleraine & District Motor Club
SIXTY-NINTH INTERNATIONAL
LSTER GRAND PRIX
CP
HIRE
Promoter:
COLERAINE & DISTRICT MOTOR CLUB LTD.
SATURDAY 22ND AUGUST 1998
enue - DUNDROD • LISBURN • CO.ANTRIM
STANNIFER
SNODDONS
ULSTER GRAND PRIX 2002
DUNDROD & DISTRICT MOTORCYCLE CLUB
Race Day Saturday 17th August
at 10.45am
(Practice Thursday 15th August at 11.00am)
ADMISSION ONLY £10/€16
ROAD
REGAL
SEVENTY-SECOND INTERNATIONA
ULSTER
GRAND PRI
STANNIFER
Snoddon
Dundrod Circuit, Lisburn, Co. An
Saturday 18th August 2001
Race Area Admission and Programme £1
Promoted by
Coleraine & District Motor Club
SIXTY-FIFTH INTERNATIONAL
ULSTER GRAND PRIX
sponsored by
Coleraine
Ballymena
Belfast
Plant Hire Ltd
promoted by
Coleraine & District Motor Club Ltd

CHAPTER 8

CRISIS? WHAT CRISIS? 1993–2002

When, in late 1992, the news broke that Ulster Centre Promotions had approached Lisburn Borough Council for a £5,000 cash injection to make up a shortfall on receipts for the event, it raised questions once again about the future of the Ulster. Most of the resultant press coverage placed the blame for the current predicament squarely on the shoulders of the organisers for their lack of enthusiasm and ability to properly market the meeting.

DONNELLAN PHOTOGRAPHIC ARCHIVES

Iain Duffus astride a 600cc Kawasaki, 2003. Duffus, from Glenrothes in Scotland, was a regular and popular visitor to the Ulster for many years. His four wins at the Prix between 1993 and 2003 were achieved riding Honda, Yamaha, and Kawasaki machines.

The Supporters' Club warned the promoters that the Ulster was on borrowed time, and that unless they made a success of it in 1993, there would be no reserves left to give them the following year.

Come February 1993, the promoters announced that the 1993 event – the 40th anniversary of the first Ulster at Dundrod – would include two races for historic bikes. While this was good news for the legion of classic bike fans, others wondered if that was really the road to go down to keep the Ulster alive.

Then in late June came a surprise from a totally unexpected quarter – a major sponsorship deal for the event by Pepsi. Although it came somewhat too late to benefit the sponsor properly, it was nevertheless a welcome development and Pepsi ended up putting quite a lot of thought and effort into their involvement, with a run of impressive publicity.

The uncertainty surrounding the UGP finally came to a head shortly after the 1993 race. First of all, the Supporters' Club informed Ulster Centre Promotions in late August that they were so dissatisfied with the way the event was being run that no further support would be given. In response, UCP announced that they would shortly disband, and no longer run the race.

Thankfully, by early October, it appeared that a solution to the crisis was imminent when Billy Nutt from the Coleraine and District Motor Club, (organisers of the North West 200), revealed his club's willingness to take over the running of the Ulster, with himself as Clerk of the Course. This suggestion had the full backing of the Supporters' Club. However, the obvious delight at this news soon evaporated when the MCUI Ulster Centre revealed that a rival bid for staging the event had been received from the owners of the Bishopscourt Racing Circuit; a bid that, if accepted, would see the Ulster move to the Downpatrick race track. The UGP Supporters' Club responded with a strongly-worded statement to say that they would wind up if the event was moved from Dundrod; a warning that was heeded by the Ulster Centre delegates at their meeting on 5 November, when they awarded the 1994 UGP to Billy Nutt and the Coleraine and District Motor Club.

After all the dust had settled, the new organising team got down to work and announced that for the 1994 programme, an additional race for Supermono single-cylinder four-stroke machines would be held. On the day, and aided, no doubt, by the favourable weather, the racing went down well with the fans, and Phillip McCallen (Honda) established yet another record by becoming the first rider to win four races in a day at the Ulster.

The Ulster Grand Prix revival continued in 1995 when Billy Nutt and the Coleraine Club succeeded in persuading Lisburn Borough Council to make further improvements to the facilities at the start and finish area, including the upgrading of the terracing and an extension to the grandstand. In addition, that year there was an almost festival-like atmosphere in the run-up to race day. Practice days had by then been moved from Wednesday and Thursday to Thursday and Friday, and when Friday's practice was over, a large crowd remained in the paddock area

EDDIE MATEER

Joey Dunlop at the Ulster, 1995. Joey wasn't called the 'King of the Road' for nothing. His record of 26 Isle of Man TT wins, 24 Ulster wins, and 13 North West 200 wins is well known by all motorcycling fans, as is his winning the TT Formula 1 World Championship 5 times from 1982 to 1986. Yet, despite his outstanding achievements, fame certainly never went to his head, for right up until his untimely death in 2000, he was still the same humble, down-to-earth guy that had ridden in his first road race at the Temple thirty years previously. In 1986, Joey was awarded the MBE for services to motorcycling sport, and ten years later, an OBE for humanitarian work for children in Romanian orphanages. In January 2015, in a poll organised by the Belfast Telegraph, *he was voted Northern Ireland's greatest ever sports star. The fifty thousand mourners who lined the road for his funeral stood in a stunned silence as the service was broadcast live by Northern Ireland television. There will never be another like him.*

ALASTAIR McCOOK

Phillip McCallen on his 250cc Honda in the holding area at the 1991 UGP. During the 1990s, McCallen was, without doubt, the man to beat. His first major success came in 1988 when he won the Lightweight Manx Grand Prix on his first attempt. Winner of no less than 11 Isle of Man TTs, 14 Ulster Grand Prix, and 5 North West 200 – including his astonishing feat in 1996 of notching up 5 UGP wins in a single day – his dashing and adventurous style of riding was sorely missed when he retired from racing in 1999.

until well after dusk, entertained by the display of vintage bikes, a car-boot sale, a chat show, and a firework display. The format for the racing itself was roughly the same as in 1994, but with the addition of a Sidecar race – the first since 1989.

During the winter of 1995 and the following spring, Lisburn Borough Council completed resurfacing and extending the area behind the grandstand, so all was ready for the 1996 Ulster. The riders' building in the paddock had also been refurbished, and further course improvements were made, including the removal of several ditches. This was the third year that the

Coleraine Club had organised the Ulster, and they had certainly found their feet. They persuaded the *Belfast Telegraph* to provide free advertising and pre-race publicity for the meeting, and after a couple of years experimenting with the timing of the practice sessions, they once more reverted to the traditional Wednesday and Thursday. The racing format was a repeat of the successful 1995 formula, and the star of the show once again was Phillip McCallen (Honda), who went one better than two years previously by winning five races – both Superbike races, both 250cc races, and the 600cc Supersport class.

More improvements were made to facilities for the 1997 meeting, with the Department of the Environment carrying out much-needed resurfacing the whole way from the Hairpin to Leathemstown. The winter months, meanwhile, were dominated by an ongoing dispute between Billy Nutt and Robert Dunlop. The latter had not been permitted to race in the North West 200 because of concerns over his fitness – Dunlop had been left with severe tendon damage after a major accident at the 1994 Isle of Man F1 TT – and he wasn't cleared to ride in the Ulster until mid-July.

Unfortunately, the date of the 1997 UGP clashed with a round of the British Supercup Championship

EDDIE MATEER

Robert Dunlop is pushed off on his 125cc Honda by his great friend and helper Liam Beckett, Dundrod, 1996. After an apprenticeship on short-circuits from the age of sixteen, Robert Dunlop went on to become one of the greatest riders the sport has known. Winner of 5 Isle of Man TTs – including the Ultra-Lightweight class in three consecutive years – 9 UGPs and 15 North West 200s, Robert would undoubtedly have surpassed that total but for a horrendous accident at the 1994 TT when the rear wheel of his Honda RC45 collapsed. Despite multiple injuries and a long lay-off, he did return to racing. Then in 1998 he won another 125cc TT, which resulted in the famous footage of him tossing away his crutches at the winners' presentation. He tragically died after crashing during practice at the 2008 North West 200.

EDDIE MATEER

DONNELLAN PHOTOGRAPHIC ARCHIVES

Top: *Phelim Owens (Honda) at the 1996 Ulster, ready to do battle in the 125cc class, which he won. Owens was one of Northern Ireland's top 125cc riders in the 1990s. Finishing on the UGP podium six years in a row, from 1994 to 1999 inclusive, and including three victories, he was always a hard man to beat.*

Bottom: *Welsh rider Jason Griffiths in action on a Yamaha Superbike, 2003. Griffiths held the UGP lap record from 1994 to 1999, and won four UGPs between 1994 and 1998, including, in 1994, the only Supermono race ever held at the Ulster.*

at Cadwell Park, which sadly affected the quality of the entry, and a plan to include in the programme an additional race for production machines had to be scrapped as insufficient entries were received.

That paled into insignificance, however, when tragedy struck on race day: during the sighting lap of the Sidecar race, an outfit, driven by Stephen Galligan and his son Aaron, veered out of control on the Flying Kilo and crashed, killing seven-year-old spectator, Christopher McConnell-Hewitt. After that, the rest of the day's activities were of little importance.

The main talking point in the early part of 1998 was an application by Davy Beattie, joint owner of Bishopscourt racetrack, to once again try to have the Ulster Grand Prix staged there. This met with the response it deserved, both from road race fans and the MCUI Ulster Centre, who stated that as long as the Coleraine Club were prepared to hold the event at Dundrod, that would be the way it would remain.

Due to the tragic spectator fatality at the 1997 Ulster, the Sidecar race was dropped from the programme, and, indeed, the class never again figured at Dundrod. The entry list for that year's meeting was a vast improvement on the previous year's and, as a result, the racing turned out to be the closest and

ALASTAIR McCOOK

DONNELLAN PHOTOGRAPHIC ARCHIVES

Left: *Owen McNally astride a 750cc Kawasaki (a bike he rarely rode) in 1998. McNally was one of the top 250cc riders in the 1990s. Riding his Aprilia, he won the UGP in 1997, 1998 and 1999. A popular, outgoing personality, he was also the Irish 125cc Road Racing champion in 1999.*

most exciting for a while.

In 1999, the racing was just as entertaining – particularly the 600cc Supersport class, which had for years provided the best racing of the meetings – although the overall entry left a lot to be desired.

In 2000, a black cloud descended on road racing. In that one year, five Northern Irish racers lost their lives to the sport – including Joey Dunlop who tragically died at Tallinn in Estonia. When Gary Dynes and Andrew McClean were killed at Monaghan less than a week before the Ulster, it looked as if the meeting at Dundrod might not take place. There were calls for the event to be boycotted and for road racing to be banned altogether. Thankfully, for the sake of the sport, the Ulster did go ahead, though few present could have really enjoyed the day, even if the racing was close and exciting. There was almost a sigh of relief at the end of the meeting because there had been no serious incidents.

A taskforce was set up in the wake of the road race fatalities of 2000, and in 2001 its presence was keenly felt in the many recommendations it made to improve safety standards. One of these decreed that all road races should provide for practice sessions on the evening before race day, and unfortunately, the organisers of the Temple and Carrowdore events found themselves unable to comply with this stipulation (in the latter case, this was mainly due to the objections of local residents).

Top: *Richard Britton (Suzuki) at Dundrod, 2003. Like many other good competitors before him, Britton, from Enniskillen, never actually won at the Ulster, but he did chalk up six podium places between 1998 and 2004. One of Ireland's most consistent road racers, he was Regal 600cc champion on four occasions.*

DONNELLAN PHOTOGRAPHIC ARCHIVES

Adrian Archibald on his Suzuki approaching Wheeler's Corner in the 2003 Ulster. Archibald, from Ballymoney, was successful at the UGP on four occasions between 2000 and 2003. Noted for his smooth riding style, he also had three victories at the Isle of Man TT, including a double for TAS Suzuki in 2003.

Then, in the early spring, there was a serious outbreak of foot-and-mouth disease across the UK, which resulted in the cancellation of most sporting fixtures, including the Cookstown, Tandragee and Dundrod 150 races, and even the North West 200.

Just as it looked as if the entire season would be wiped out, the Mid-Antrim 150 and the Ulster were given the green light to go ahead. Possibly due to the lack of action over the summer, the Ulster turned out to be one of the best supported for many years. There was a record number of entries, and car parks and vantage points were crammed full on both practice and race days.

Not long after the 2001 Prix, Billy Nutt requested a meeting with the officials of the Supporters' Club at which he informed them that due to the pressure caused by all the serious incidents that had occurred during his time at the helm, he had decided to call it a day. The Supporters' Club were naturally disappointed, but respected his decision, though they were bitterly upset when Nutt refused them a stand at the Odyssey Motorcycle Show because they had criticised him for saying that road racing should end.

ALASTAIR McCOOK

David Jefferies speaks to the press after winning the first Superbike race on his V&M Yamaha at the 1999 Ulster. Jeffries, an affable Yorkshireman, was Archibald's TAS Suzuki teammate and a determined, adventurous, and supremely talented competitor. A four-time winner of the Ulster Grand Prix, and nine-time winner of the Isle of Man TT, Jefferies was the first to win three races during the week-long Manx Festival for three consecutive years.

The Coleraine Club then announced that without Billy Nutt they could not provide the manpower necessary for running the Ulster.

The situation looked bleak. For a while it appeared as if a consortium comprised of officials from other racing clubs would make a bid to run the 2002 meeting, but in early December, the Dundrod & District Motorcycle Club offered to take on the responsibility, and their bid was accepted.

So ended several turbulent years for the Ulster Grand Prix. Would things ever run smoothly for this much-loved race?

ULSTER GRAND PRIX 2003
DUNDROD & DISTRICT MOTORCYCLE CLUB
IN ASSOCIATION WITH
Race Day Saturday 16th August
(Practice Thursday 14th August)
PROGRAMME & ADMISSION ONLY £10/€15
S.B.E.
SOLITUDE MOTORS
Stena Line
ULSTER GRAND PRIX 2004
BIKE WEEK
IN ASSOCIATION WITH
16th-21st
AUGUST 2004
BIKE WEEK
IN ASSOCIATION WITH
8th-13th
AUGUST 2005
PROGRAMME & ADMISSION ONLY £15/€25
ULSTER GRAND PRIX 2006
BIKE WEEK
IN ASSOCIATION WITH
LISBURN CITY COUNCIL
14TH - 19TH
AUGUST 2006
PROGRAMME & ADMISSION ONLY £15/€25
JESTER
ROAD RACING IRELAND
THE ULSTER GRAND PRIX
POWERED BY
BELFAST TELEGRAPH
12TH-18TH AUGUST 2007
PROGRAMME & ADMISSION
ONLY £15/€25
IN ASSOCIATION WITH
LISBURN CITY COUNCIL
BELFAST TELEGRAPH
MILENCO
BBC SPORT NI
Pacemaker Press
£15/€20
THE ULSTER GRAND PRIX
POWERED BY
Belfast Telegraph
OFFICIAL 2008
SOUVENIR PROGRAMME
www.ulstergrandprix.org
LISBURN CITY COUNCIL
BIKE WEEK
AUGUST 11-16th
DUNDROD CIRCUIT
STONEYFORD CONCRETE
GP ULSTER GRAND PRIX
£10/€12
OFFICIAL PROGR
The World's
Fastest Road Race
9TH - 15TH AUGUST 2009
McKINSTRY
GP ULSTER GRAND PRIX
OFFICIAL
PROGRAMME
The World's
Fastest Road Race™
McKINSTRY
GP ULSTER GRAND PRIX
OFFICIAL
PROGRAMME
2011
The World's
Fastest Road Race™
www.ulstergrandprix.net
90th 1922
The World's
Fastest Road Race

CHAPTER 9

BIKE WEEK BECKONS 2003–2012

Shortly after the 2002 UGP, on 22 August 2002, officers from the Supporters' Club met with the new organisers to hold a post-mortem on the event and to discuss ways things could be improved – as they had done over the years with Ulster Centre Promotions and the Coleraine Club.

Darren Lindsay on the Nibbles Suzuki in the 2003 UGP. Lindsay's home was on the Dundrod circuit, which no doubt was a help in his performances at the Ulster. Between 2002 and 2006 he was successful five times, and also had two wins at the Manx Grand Prix.

DONNELLAN PHOTOGRAPHIC ARCHIVES

DONNELLAN PHOTOGRAPHIC ARCHIVES

New Zealander Bruce Anstey on the TAS Suzuki Superbike at the 2003 Ulster. One of the most approachable and popular riders in any paddock, Anstey is a 13-time winner at the Ulster (his first was in 2003, his last in 2017), has been victorious on 12 occasions at the Isle of Man TT, and 10 times at the North West 200. In every season from 2002 to 2015 he has finished in the top three at all of the IOM TTs, UGPs, and North West 200s that took place – an incredible record.

Unlike former occasions, however, this meeting led to a major fallout when an accusation was made that representatives of the Supporters' Club had misappropriated a substantial amount of Grand Prix funds. The matter was reported to the police and the accused – men who had worked tirelessly for the Ulster Grand Prix for many years – had to seek legal advice. They were eventually completely exonerated, receiving apologies and legal costs, however they felt that they could no longer work to raise money for the Prix, particularly as those who had made such serious allegations against them were still involved in running the race. Fortunately, for the sake of the Ulster, others in the Supporters' Club took up the reins.

After all the uncertainty of late 2002, the 2003 Ulster turned out to be a success, with no serious accidents occurring throughout the day. The one notable fact about the meeting was the appearance, for the first time, of rider John McGuinness (Yamaha), who finished third in the 600cc production race.

For 2004, the Dundrod Club announced that they were organising an 'Ulster Grand Prix Bike Week', which incorporated the Dundrod 150 races, to be run after Thursday's practice sessions. In the event, the weather decided otherwise, and a combination of torrential rain and low cloud on both Wednesday and Thursday played havoc with their plans.

Wednesday's practice was completely wiped out, and Thursday's Dundrod 150 races were also cancelled. Thursday's practice did go ahead, but riders were only allowed five laps – and all of these untimed. The elements relented for race day itself, but once more tragedy struck the sport when, during the first race of the day, the 1000cc Production Race, rider Andy Wallace (Suzuki) was killed in a five-bike pile up at the exit from Wheeler's Corner. Three other races were red-flagged during the course

DONNELLAN PHOTOGRAPHIC ARCHIVES

John McGuinness on the HM Plant Honda Superbike, 2006. Next to Joey Dunlop, John McGuinness is without question the most successful road racer there has been. Winner of twenty-three TTs, he has, however, been less successful at the Ulster, especially in more recent years. His first appearance at the Ulster was in 2003, and in 2005 he won two races at Dundrod. Since then his visits to the Ulster have been sporadic and have not produced any further victories.

Martin Finnegan in action on a Supersport Honda during the 2006 Ulster. Born in Lusk, County Dublin, Finnegan graduated from grasstrack racing to become a popular and successful road racer, winning over forty Irish road races during his career. A trophy in his honour is still awarded each year at the Isle of Man TT to the Irish rider who records the fastest lap.

DONNELLAN PHOTOGRAPHIC ARCHIVES

of the afternoon, race distances were shortened, and the final Superbike race was cancelled due to lack of time.

In 2005, despite all the problems encountered the previous year, the Dundrod Club decided to continue with the Bike Week formula, and once again scheduled four Dundrod 150 national races for the Thursday afternoon when practice ended. That year, however, they were more fortunate with the weather, and all events ran on time. The six-race programme that year also saw the reintroduction, for the first time since 1988, of a Superstock race – a class that would become a regular feature of the Ulster, and nearly always a closely-fought one at that.

The same race programme was announced for 2006 – the Bike Week format was beginning to look like the established pattern for the future of the meeting – and the circuit itself had never looked in better shape. Since the Dundrod Club had taken over the running of the Ulster, vast improvements had been made to the spectator and competitor facilities around the paddock and grandstand areas. But more importantly, the club had introduced important safety measures around the circuit, including continual resurfacing – the entire stretch of the course from Quarterlands to the Hairpin had been resurfaced for the 2006 event – the provision of lots of additional safety bales and the removal of dangerous posts and other hazardous features. No doubt this had an effect on the speeds recorded, with no fewer than five riders lapping faster than the 130 mph barrier for the first time.

The image of the event had improved considerably under the club's ministrations but, obviously, this had cost a great deal of money. So it came as no surprise when, in March 2007, the organisers announced that unless a substantial amount of assistance was forthcoming, either through government funding or backing from private enterprise, there was a definite possibility that the Ulster would not be held that year. Happily, the uncertainty ended on 26 June when it was revealed that the *Belfast Telegraph* would sponsor the event, providing cash, plus editorial and promotional support. The Ulster went ahead as planned.

In 2008, the *Belfast Telegraph* remained on board as title sponsor and things were again beginning to look promising for the UGP. There had

DONNELLAN PHOTOGRAPHIC ARCHIVES

Ryan Farquhar (Kawasaki) leads Bruce Anstey (Suzuki) into Wheeler's Corner in the 2009 Ulster. It's hard to believe that Farquhar first stood on the UGP podium as long ago as 1997, and until a serious accident ended his illustrious career in 2016, he had amassed nine wins at the UGP and three in the Isle of Man TT. Farquhar was largely responsible for the introduction of the Supertwin class, which is now firmly established on the racing scene, and his 357 race wins has been recognised by Guinness World Records.

Guy Martin on the AIM Racing Yamaha on the stretch between Joey's and Jordan's Cross, 2006. This is my favourite part of the Dundrod circuit. Not only does it offer a good vantage point for the racing, but when the weather is fine, having a view like this of Lough Neagh makes the day rather special.

DONNELLAN PHOTOGRAPHIC ARCHIVES

DONNELLAN PHOTOGRAPHIC ARCHIVES

It's not often a photographer is fortunate enough to get a shot like this. Gary Johnson, here seen in action at the 2010 UGP on the AIM Racing Suzuki, never won at Dundrod, but finished on the podium on four occasions between 2009 and 2013, as well as winning twice at the Isle of Man TT in 2011 and 2014.

been a noticeable increase in pre-race publicity in 2007 and 2008, and the scene was set for another enthralling spectacle of speed.

Alas, it was not to be, for Saturday, 16 August 2008 was one of the wettest days at Dundrod since the Ulster moved there in 1953. The rain, which began just before road-closing, got heavier and heavier, and there was standing water all around the circuit. In fact, on the approach to Wheeler's Corner, the water was gushing out on to the road like a mini waterfall. So relentless was the rain that Clerk of the Course Noel Johnston had no alternative but to abort the day's proceedings without a wheel being turned. Most reports say that the Ulster Grand Prix had been wiped out in its entirety for the first time ever. This was, strictly speaking, not correct, for the 125cc

DONNELLAN PHOTOGRAPHIC ARCHIVES

William Dunlop on his Yamaha during the 2010 Ulster. William, son of Robert Dunlop, started racing in 2000 when he was fifteen years of age, and during his career won more than one hundred Irish national road races. His first podium at the UGP was in 2005 when he finished second to John McGuinness in the 250cc class, and overall he won at the Ulster seven times. A stylish rider if ever there was one, the world was shocked beyond belief when, in 2018, he became the third member of the Dunlop dynasty to be tragically killed while racing.

race which Ian Lougher (Honda) won on the Thursday was actually an Ulster Grand Prix race, and not a Dundrod 150 event.

Doubts over the running of the 2009 meeting were soon dispelled when it was announced that, despite the loss incurred over the 2008 disaster, the organisers had applied for a date, and were determined to continue. There were two innovations that year: the inclusion in the meeting for the first time of the Supertwin class, which brought a welcome variety to the programme;

Ian Lougher (Honda) follows William Dunlop (Honda) into Wheeler's Corner, 2010. Lougher's racing career began in his native South Wales in 1982, and unbelievably is still going strong. He has won the UGP on eighteen occasions – his first in 1998. His first podium at the Ulster was in the 400cc Supersport event of 1989; his last was in the 2018 Supertwin race, and incredibly he was still mixing it with the leaders in 2019. In recognition of his long-standing support and love for the Ulster, the corner on the Dundrod circuit between Ireland's and Joey's was named after him in 2009.

DONNELLAN PHOTOGRAPHIC ARCHIVES

and the introduction of a new system of spectator admission charges.

The cost of a wristband that would grant access to the circuit for the whole of race week was £10, though this was slightly offset by reducing the price of the race programme from £15 to £10. In subsequent years the cost of the wristband was increased to £15, then to £25, while the race programme was further reduced to £5 – surely still a small price to pay for such exciting entertainment!

It almost seems an annual occurrence that uncertainty surfaces regarding the future of the Ulster, and 2010 was no exception. The organisers had been promised £50,000 from the Department of Culture, Arts and Leisure for essential maintenance and safety improvements at Dundrod and had spent that amount in anticipation. In addition to the main grandstand, three other grandstands had been erected at Leathemstown, the Hairpin and Dawson's Bend; and large-screen viewing and live-streaming on the internet were to be provided. By the spring, however, the funding had fallen through and concerns grew that the event would have to be cancelled. Thankfully, the local council stepped in to help with the shortfall, and the event went ahead.

For a welcome change, the main talking point in relation to the 2011 meeting was the racing itself. For the main Superbike race, Bruce Anstey (Honda) had qualified poorly, and was forced to start in the second group. Come Saturday, however, Bruce found pace from somewhere and won on corrected time, even though Guy Martin (Suzuki) had been first to take the chequered flag. It was truly a bizarre situation, and one that caused a great deal of discussion and controversy.

Thankfully the 2012 meeting, which was the 90th anniversary of the first Ulster Grand Prix, passed off with no controversy on or off the track.

DONNELLAN PHOTOGRAPHIC ARCHIVES

Conor Cummins on a Superstock Yamaha on his first visit to Dundrod in 2006. Born in Douglas in the Isle of Man, Cummins has turned out to be, in many fans' estimation, the best Manx solo road racer ever. He became a professional rider in 2006 and quickly established himself as a force to be reckoned with. His first podium at the UGP was the following year, and the first of his two Ulster wins occurred in 2009 with a Superbike victory on a Kawasaki.

OFFICIAL PROGRAMME 2013
The World's Fastest Road Race™
www.ulstergrandprix.net
£5
The World's Fastest Road Race™
GP ULSTER GRAND PRIX 2014
METZELER
11th - 16th AUGUST 2014
£5
ULSTER GRAND PRIX 2015
The World's Fastest Road Race™
PROGRAMME • 3rd - 8th AUGUST 2015
mce insurance
GP ULSTER GRAND PRIX
The World's Fastest Road Race
BIKE WEEK PROGRAMME • 8th - 13th AUGUST 2016
fona CAB
GP ULSTER GRAND PRIX
INSIDE
interviews
stats
race info
rider profiles
£10
2019
BIKE WEEK PROGRAMME 5th - 10th AUGUST 2019
www.ulstergrandprix.net
£5
The World's Fastest Road Race
BIKE WEEK PROGRAMME 6th - 12th AUGUST 2017
BIKE WEEK PROGRAMME 5th - 11th AUGUST 2018

CHAPTER 10

APPROACHING THE CENTENARY 2013–2022

The approach to the 2013 Ulster was unusually upbeat as it was announced at the launch that tyre company Metzeler were to be the new main sponsor. This was certainly a major boost for the event, especially as Metzeler promised to continue the arrangement until 2015. This year, 2013, also happened to be the 60th anniversary of the Grand Prix moving from Clady to Dundrod, and the 50th anniversary of the formation of the Ulster Grand Prix Supporters' Club; further causes for celebration.

Guy Martin in action on the Hydrax Honda in the Superbike race of 2009. Martin is regarded as something of a cult hero among racing fans. Always surrounded by legions of admirers, yet seemingly uncomfortable with all the adulation, he is, in some people's eyes, something of an eccentric. Nevertheless, he was a first-class road racer; probably the best never to have won a TT, despite accumulating seventeen podium finishes. His favourite circuit was Dundrod, where he thrilled the fans on many occasions. He won there eleven times. Since his withdrawal from racing he has become equally famous on television for attempting records on various modes of transport, other engineering-based projects and documentary programmes.

DONNELLAN PHOTOGRAPHIC ARCHIVES

After a long spell of hot, sunny weather it was almost inevitable that it would come to an end just in time for the race, and, sure enough, it rained so heavily on the Thursday afternoon of race week that the entire Dundrod 150 race programme had to be cancelled. Unfortunately for spectator attendance figures, weather forecasters predicted that Saturday would be no different, but after a dull start came periods of bright sunshine for the duration of racing, and the fans who had ignored the harbingers of a washout were rewarded with close and exciting racing.

In 2014, due to ever-increasing health and safety demands, more areas around the circuit were deemed off-limits to the public, but at least this was offset by the provision of additional grandstands at various points on the circuit.

This was also the year in which the Supporters' Club contributions to the race passed £1 million – a simply astonishing achievement, and one that was recognised by Lisburn City Council at a reception held for current and former officials of the club on 10 March 2014.

It was also around this time that a three-year funding package came from the Northern Ireland Tourist Board to enable the Dundrod Club to further grow and develop the event.

The club put this to good use with a planned extension to the paddock complex to provide a motor-home park and facilities for campers; a larger grandstand (albeit a temporary one as the old structure was becoming a safety hazard); and most importantly, the building and opening of the new David Wood Grand Prix House, which would provide a purpose-built headquarters for the race. This new building was a long overdue replacement for the old UGP House that had been erected in 1965 at the old start/finish line and had stood until its demolition in 1992.

By 2016 Metzeler had ended their three-year sponsorship of the UGP, but the Dundrod Club had moved quickly and agreed a similar contract for that year with MCE Insurance as main title sponsor. The club also announced, early in March 2016, a revised schedule for Bike Week that would allow for two extra hours of practice on the Wednesday, plus an additional thirty minutes on the Thursday. This extra thirty minutes was to facilitate a new venture being introduced for the main Superbike race: a Superpole session. Copying the British Superbike format, the plan was for the ten fastest Superbike qualifiers in practice to each have a further two laps to determine grid positions for the race.

As it turned out, Thursday's bad weather led to the postponement of

DONNELLAN PHOTOGRAPHIC ARCHIVES

Michael Dunlop (Yamaha) competing in his typically determined style during the 2009 UGP. Michael is the younger brother of William Dunlop, and he first rode in the Ulster Grand Prix in 2006. A year later, he recorded his first podium placing at the meeting. Michael is widely regarded as being one of the most aggressive and tenacious competitors in motorcycle racing and has six Ulster wins to his credit. It is somewhat of a surprise, though, that he hasn't won at the meeting since 2013. To date, he has won twenty-one times at the Isle of Man TT, and in 2016 he became the first rider to lap the 37.73 miles TT course in under seventeen minutes. Michael also holds another unique record in that he has won the TT on six different makes of machines: Honda, Kawasaki, Suzuki, Yamaha, BMW and Paton.

ALASTAIR McCOOK

Ian Hutchinson (otherwise known as 'The Bingley Bullet') tips his Milwaukee Yamaha into Tornagrough, 2014. Hutchinson has been victorious at the UGP on nine occasions, stretching from 2007 to 2016, when he won four races. He is also a sixteen-time winner at the Isle of Man TT, including an incredible feat in 2010 when he won five races to break Phillip McCallen's 1996 record of four wins. But for an accident at Silverstone later that year, in which he suffered horrendous injuries to his left leg, there is little doubt that he would have had far more successes.

this innovation until Saturday morning, following which, reaction was suitably mixed. Some thought it added more excitement to the proceedings, while others felt it achieved nothing. It could be argued that the latter opinion was more accurate, for Michael Dunlop (BMW) had been quickest in practice but been upstaged by Bruce Anstey (Honda) in the Superpole session, and when the race itself got underway, Bruce failed to make a good start and was only fourth heading down the Flying Kilo.

Following the success of the 2016 meeting, the UGP organisers received a substantial grant of £200,000 from the Northern Ireland Department of Communities to implement further health and safety improvements and provide better access facilities in the paddock for fans with disabilities. Some of the grant was also used to build a new scrutineering bay. The grant was particularly welcome, coming as it did during a continuing period of austerity.

For the 2017 Ulster, MCE Insurance were once again on board as main title sponsors, and the Charles Hurst Group took over as overall sponsors of the Dundrod 150 races on the Thursday of race week. Overnight rain caused a slight delay to the start of Saturday's racing, but as the day progressed, conditions steadily improved. The delay, however, resulted in cancellation of the Superbike Superpole session scheduled for Saturday morning, so the jury was still out on that one.

Then in September 2017, Clerk of the Course Noel Johnston announced significant changes for 2018 race week. First, that the Dundrod 150 national races which traditionally ran on the Thursday would be replaced by additional Ulster Grand Prix races. Second, the Superpole experiment was being shelved (no surprise really) and would be replaced on the Saturday morning with an extended warm-up session. The idea was that this would improve safety by enabling riders to get used to the conditions at the actual time of racing. Third, in order to cater for the many national licence holders who would be disappointed at the axing of the Dundrod 150 races, the Supertwin and Lightweight/Ultra-Lightweight

ROWLAND WHITE

Lincolnshire rider Ivan Lintin on his Kawasaki, 2015. Lintin first rode in the UGP in 2007 and has won the Supertwin class at Dundrod on three occasions. He has also won the same class twice at the Isle of Man TT. At the 2018 Southern 100 meeting, Ivan suffered severe injuries, and his life hung in the balance for a while. Happily he has made an excellent recovery.

races would be opened to both national and international licence holders.

For many years pre-race publicity for the Ulster had emphasised the fact that it was the fastest road race in the world, but this title was snatched from it at the 2018 Isle of Man TT when Peter Hickman (BMW) recorded a lap at 135.452 mph, beating the 134.614 mph Dean Harrison (Kawasaki) had achieved at Dundrod in 2017. Any chance of reclaiming the title evaporated when the weather failed to cooperate at the 2018 Prix.

In 2019, however, Peter Hickman (BMW) lapped Dundrod at an astonishing 136.415 mph, and ended up winning no less than seven races during the meeting, including five on the Saturday to equal Phillip McCallen's record set in 1996.

The dust had not long settled on the 2019 event when dire reports of a major financial crisis facing the organisers appeared in the media. Their already precarious financial position had been dealt a further blow due to low spectator turnout on the Saturday of race week – no doubt, the severe weather warning forecast had played a significant part in this. Reports circulated that the Dundrod Club were almost £300,000 in the red and that riders had not been paid the prize money due to them the very future of the Ulster looked bleak indeed.

ROWLAND WHITE

Top: *Lee Johnston (BMW) on his way to victory in 2015, when he was 'Man of the Meeting', with no less than three wins. Johnston hails from Maguiresbridge in County Fermanagh, and while he may be only 5ft 4in, he is a giant when it comes to road racing. His bubbly personality enlivens any paddock. Lee first competed at the Ulster in 2012, and right away signalled his ability by finishing third in one of the Supersport 600 races. In 2019 he achieved his ambition with his maiden victory at the Isle of Man TT.*

Right: *Derek McGee in action during the 2017 meeting. McGee, from Mullingar in County Westmeath, made his breakthrough in 2011 when he won the Irish Support Road Race Championship. He competed in the UGP for the first time in 2013, and the following year made it on to the podium with second place in the Supertwin class. In 2015 he won the Supertwin event, which is his only Ulster victory to date.*

ALASTAIR McCOOK

ALASTAIR McCOOK

Christian Elkin on his Moto3 Honda, 2018. Elkin first made his name in short-circuit racing when he was crowned British 125cc Champion in 2004 and 2005. His debut at the Ulster Grand Prix took place in 2009 when he finished third in the 125cc class behind Ian Lougher and Michael Dunlop, and since then he has gone on to notch up four victories at the Ulster, the last one as recently as 2019.

ALASTAIR McCOOK

Adam McLean aboard his 600cc Supersport Kawasaki in 2018. The local rider made his Ulster debut in 2015, and two years later took his first podium with a third place in the Supertwin event. He did even better in 2018, taking the win in the same class, but his career was on hold for some time due to an accident at the Tandragee 100 in 2019.

A birds-eye view of Dean Harrison on the Silicone Engineering Superbike Kawasaki, 2018. Harrison, from Bradford, began his road racing career in the 2010 Irish Support Championships before making his first appearance at the UGP in 2012. His first podium was in the 2014 Superstock race, which he followed up with two Ulster wins in 2017 and 2018. His three victories at the Isle of Man TT include one in 2014, just a few days after his father, Conrad, won the Sidecar TT.

ALASTAIR McCOOK

Despite talks with local politicians and other public representatives about a rescue plan, nothing emerged to save the 2020 UGP, which, as it turned out, would have been cancelled anyway because of the coronavirus outbreak. Unfortunately, the governing body, MCUI (Ulster Centre), have been disappointingly silent during this period of crisis.

Towards the end of 2020, the gloom appeared to lift a little and news filtered through that negotiations were underway that would ensure the future of the race, and that a potential title sponsor had been secured. But things went quiet again and the coronavirus pandemic led to the cancellation of most local motorsport for a second year running.

Finally, after almost a year of waiting, it was announced in November 2021 that a new organisation known as the Revival Racing Motorcycle Club – with North West 200 event director Mervyn White, and TT, North West 200 and UGP winner Phillip McCallen at the helm – had secured a rescue package of £800,000 from the Northern Ireland Executive to ensure that the centenary event in 2022 would take place.

Then, in early March 2022, came the devastating news that Tourism NI had refused to support the level of funding agreed and the event was cancelled. It was a huge disappointment and a massive blow to the sport.

Nevertheless, there is much to celebrate in the one hundred years of the Ulster Grand Prix. Since the early days of road racing, most of the all-time greats of the sport have taken part in this magnificent sporting occasion. Riders like Joe Craig, Wal Handley, Stanley Woods, Jimmie Guthrie and Walter Rusk were stars before racing was interrupted by the Second World War, and over the years since, the Ulster has played host to legends such as Artie Bell, Les Graham, Geoff Duke, John Surtees, Jim Redman, Carlo Ubbiali, Phil Read, Bill Ivy, Mike Hailwood, Giacomo Agostini, Tom Herron, Ray McCullough, Carl Fogarty, Steve Hislop, Brian Reid, Phillip McCallen, Guy Martin and the Dunlops (Joey, Robert, William and Michael). The list is endless.

The Ulster has been through significant trials during its history, yet it has always succeeded in overcoming the obstacles in its path. Hopefully, it will rise once more from the ashes, and in the years ahead, many more names will be added to the illustrious list of riders who have graced the roads of Clady and Dundrod.

ALASTAIR McCOOK

Peter Hickman in action on the 675cc Supersport Triumph, 2018. When Hickman arrived at Dundrod in 2014 for his debut at the UGP, no one could have foreseen that in a few short years he would rip up the record books. His first victory came the following year in the Superbike race, and he went on to record three more in 2017, two in 2018, and an astonishing seven in 2019, including five on the Saturday's programme to finally equal Phillip McCallen's feat of 1996. Into the bargain, in the Thursday Superbike race, he lapped Dundrod at 136.415 mph, which is a far cry from the first Dundrod lap record set in 1953 by Geoff Duke and Ken Kavanagh at 91.74 mph. Hickman is no slouch on the short-circuit scene either, having finished sixth in the 2019 British Superbike Championship and fifth in 2021.

PRICE, 6D. EACH.

PROGRAMME.

THE ULSTER MOTOR CYCLE CLUB.

GRAND PRIX.

140 MILES HANDICAP ROAD RACE

(Seven Laps of 20 Miles each),

SATURDAY, 14TH OCTOBER, 1922.

OFFICIALS:

Chief Marshals—W. J. Chambers and G. Bowman.

Starters—W. Simms and S. J. Brownlee.

Judges—T. Moles, Esq., M.P., Mr. Miscampbell, Junr., J. J. Kennedy, R. Condell, A. Waddell and S. Hutchinson.

Timekeepers—R. M'Lardy, J. Millar, W. Kearney, W. Wright and J. Stewart.

Machine Stewards—W. J. White, J. Boston and W. Dowling.

Depot Marshals—R. G. Lindsay and A. Waddell.

Hon. Secretary—R. G. Lindsay, 5 Cross Avenue, Marlborough Park, Belfast.

Hon. Treasurer—A. Waddell, 29 Claremont Street, Belfast.

Hon. Trials Secretary—W. Dowling, 48 Candahar Street, Belfast.

Chairman on Committee—J. Boston.

Race Secretary—W. J. White, c/o. J. W. Shaw & Co., Chichester Street, Belfast.

Marshals of the Course will wear White Armlets.

And the Stewards	,,	Blue Armlets.
Despatch Riders	,,	Old Gold.
Chief Marshals	,,	Helio.
Machine Stewards	,,	Green.
Depot Marshals	,,	Pink.
Depot Attendants	,,	Pink Ribbon.

The decision of the Committee on all matters is final.

In addition to Prizes already offered, a Trophy has been presented to the Club by the Anglo-American, Shell Mex, and British Petroleum Oil Co., to be known as THE ULSTER GRAND PRIX TROPHY; to be awarded to the winner and held by him for one year only. This Trophy to be competed for annually in this particular event.

In this race, Mr. J. W. Shaw has very kindly presented a Gold Medal for the Competitor who, in the opinion of the Judges, displays most pluck and endurance in the race; to be won in the same manner as the Nesbitt Trophy in the Isle of Man T.T.

Official Car will traverse the Course announcing start of race at 12-45, and will leave starting point at this time; and will again announce Course open at termination of race. Until such time no traffic or spectators will be allowed to trespass the Course.

The Club has gone to a considerable amount of trouble and expense to try and make this an annual event, and earnestly appeal to spectators to assist the Marshals by keeping the Course clear, especially at corners and at starting point, so as to give the Competitors a fair chance and avoid accidents.

Wm. Brown & Sons (Belfast), Ltd., Printers

PROGRAMME PARADE

THE STORY OF THE UGP RACE PROGRAMME

In October 1922, when the officials of the Ulster Motorcycle Club sat down to produce a programme for the very first Ulster Grand Prix, they could hardly have imagined that the practice would last for a hundred years … and hopefully will continue for many more. Mind you, that initial production would not have taken a great deal in the way of effort. Printed by Wm. Brown & Sons, Belfast, and selling at 6d (2½p), it was a simple piece of green card folded in half, containing lists of officials, prizes, competitors and their machines, as well as a lap chart.

Yet from such modest beginnings, the programme quickly blossomed into a veritable treasure-trove of reading material, so much so that by 1925 it was 84 pages long; and by 1927, a staggering 152 pages – and still costing only 6d. How's that for a bargain? The articles contained in the programmes in those early years make interesting reading even today, with titles such as 'The Growth of Road Racing', 'The Inner Meaning of the Grand Prix', and 'The Persecution of the Motor Cyclist'.

The importance of the race as a tourist attraction in the late 1920s is reflected by the amount of space in the programmes devoted to promoting Northern Ireland in general, with articles such as 'Ulster for the Angler' and 'The Pride of the World – The Story of Belfast's Shipbuilding Industry'. Indeed, of the forty-eight photographs included in the 1929 programme, no less than forty depict local scenic views. It might also surprise you to learn that two of Ulster's most eminent literary talents contributed articles to the UGP programme. In 1927, playwright and dramatist St John Ervine described the attractions of the Antrim coast, while Lynn C. Doyle, author of *An Ulster Childhood* and *Ballygullion*, shared with readers some of the delights of his native County Down.

In 1929, the programme, still containing 100 pages, rose in price to 1s 0d (5p); a figure that was maintained through to 1939 when the Second World War interrupted proceedings.

A watershed year for the UGP programme came in 1930, when not only was its page size standardised at

9 by 6 inches (a format that was also to last through the decade), but the reading matter unmistakably shifted from an emphasis on tourism to the sport itself. This must have been a welcome development for the enthusiasts of the time, especially as there were articles by high-calibre writers such R.H. Wright (former president of the MCUI and, for many years, chief timekeeper of the Ulster), and Graham Walker (winner of the Senior UGP in 1926, 1928 and 1929, and later a well-known and much-loved, broadcaster and journalist). These two men were frequent contributors to the programme over a long period. Both wrote their first articles for the 1930 publication, and both were still going strong right into the mid-1950s.

One of the pages in the 1937 programme contained a large laurel wreath surrounded by a black border, and was dedicated to the memory of Jimmy Guthrie, who had been tragically killed in the German Grand Prix a fortnight before. It was a striking tribute to the Scottish ace who had won the 1935 Senior UGP when it had been awarded the title of Grand Prix d'Europe.

It was in the late 1930s that the possibility of a 100 mph lap began to feature prominently as a topic of interest. Until 1939 that is, when Walter Rusk and Dorino Serafini removed the need for further speculation on the subject, and Adolf Hitler, showing a total lack of consideration, denied everyone the opportunity to celebrate the achievement in print the following year.

When the Prix (and the programme)

resumed in 1947, the price had gone up to 1s 6d (7½p), and the page size had increased to 9.5 by 7.5 inches. The new format was intended to bridge the transition from Clady to Dundrod, and it lasted right through to 1954. In the meantime, however, there were two further price increases: in 1948 to 2s 0d (10p); and in 1951 to 2s 6d (12½p).

One of the main features in the programmes of the immediate post-war era was a competitors' 'Who's Who', which gave brief biographical details of all the participating riders – a task that in 1948 took up all of eighteen pages. These pen portraits soon became an established part of the format, continuing right through the 1950s, and surviving until 1964, albeit in a greatly condensed form. They did make a fleeting comeback in 1969/70 before disappearing from the scene for good.

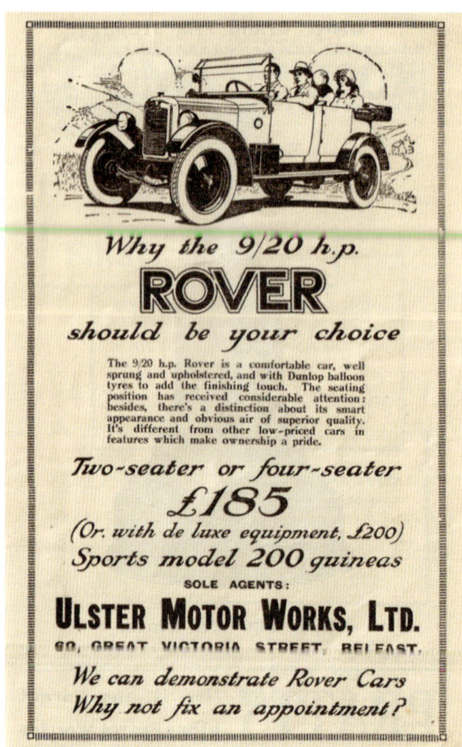

In 1955, fans were treated to yet another new style of programme: the pocket-sized edition, which measured approximately 8.5 by 5.5 inches. This appeared to be a popular enough choice as, with slight modification, it stood the test of time for twenty-two years. The price, on the other hand, didn't quite make it through the same period unscathed. The 2s 6d cover charge that was first introduced in 1951 managed to escape alteration until 1969 (not a bad record) when it underwent a modest adjustment to 3s 0d (15p). Unfortunately, the ravages of inflation during the 1970s hit particularly hard, and the programme suffered a series of increases: 20p in 1971, 30p in 1973, 50p in 1976, and 60p in 1977.

The late 1960s and most of the 1970s proved to be a very lean time for the UGP programme, with few articles of genuine interest. The exceptions to that were those written by the late Billy McMaster, who was an absolute genius when it came to putting pen to paper. His annual contributions, stretching from 1947 to 1985, placed him head and shoulders above everyone else. His inimitable style, which was both informative and entertaining, lifted the UGP programme, and his untimely death in 1986 was a terrible blow to many facets of motorcycle sport.

In 1978, the responsibility for compiling and producing the race programme was entrusted to the Supporters' Club, and a larger size of 11.5 by 8 inches was adopted. The quality and variety of the literary content improved dramatically under their management, and colour photographs were introduced for the first time. This led to an increased asking price of £1, which rose to £2 in 1981, and to £3 in 1986 as printing costs soared. In 1994, it increased again, to £5, while 1999 ushered in the first-ever £10 asking price. This was further increased to £12 the following year, a change that almost sparked a revolt by the Supporters' Club personnel responsible for selling the programmes on race day as it meant having to give change, and consequently slowed things up considerably. As a result, in 2001, the price was reduced to £10.

When the Dundrod & District Motorcycle Club took over organisation of the race in 2002, they also assumed responsibility for the race programme, which gradually became a more

professionally produced publication, due in no small measure to the advent of more sophisticated computer technology. With the arrival of the Ulster Grand Prix Bike Week in 2004, the price was increased to £15 (though this included admission to the circuit), but was subsequently reduced to £10 in 2009, and to £5 the following year due to the fact that spectators now had to pay an admission charge. In 2018, the price rose to £10 once more.

However, that is a small amount to pay, especially for those fans who count programme collecting among their hobbies. Issues from past Ulsters

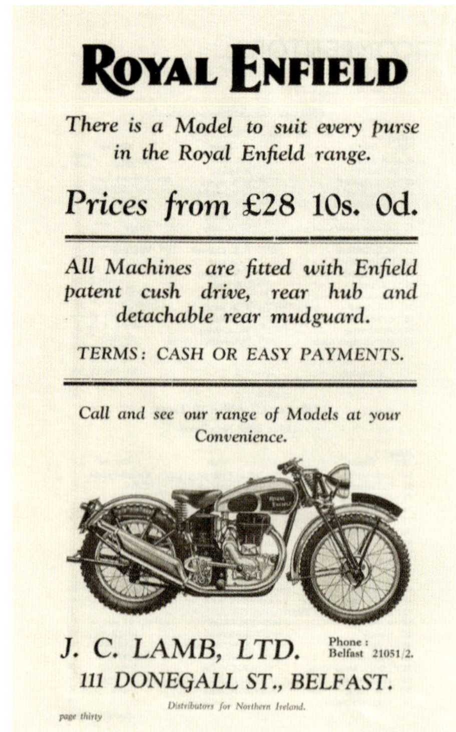

are eagerly sought after – particularly those from the 1920s and 1930s, which are now rare and hard to come by.

All in all, the programme is an iconic part of the UGP experience. The articles, statistics, and even the adverts themselves, all combine to capture the atmosphere of each race day and provide spectators with a much-loved memento of the event.

fona
CAB
GP ULSTER GRAND PRIX
INSIDE
interviews
stats
race info
rider profiles
£10
2019
BIKE WEEK PROGRAMME 5th - 10th AUGUST 2019
www.ulstergrandprix.net
ISSN 2044-9712

APPENDIX 1

RACE RECORDS

1922–39 inclusive, races held on the original Clady circuit (20.5 miles to the lap)

1922 **14 October**

		Average speed (mph)
Handicap Event		
1st	H.W. Hassall (Norton)	60.57
2nd	F. Andrews (Trump-JAP)	49.65
3rd	J.F. Dinsmore (Norton)	57.59
Class Winners		
Over 600cc	N.P. Metcalfe (Brough-Superior)	55.38
600cc	H.W. Hassall (Norton)	60.57
350cc	F. Andrews (Trump-JAP)	49.65
250cc	W.L. Handley (OK Junior)	52.39
Fastest Lap	H. Langman (Scott)	65.70

1923 **15 September**

Handicap Event		
1st	W.L. Handley (Rex-Acme)	55.95
2nd	J.W. Shaw (Zenith-JAP)	60.02
3rd	J. Craig (Norton)	62.99
Class Winners		
Over 600cc	No finishers	/
600cc	J. Craig (Norton)	62.99
350cc	J.W. Shaw (Zenith-JAP)	60.02
250cc	W.L. Handley (Rex-Acme)	55.95
Fastest Lap	J. Whalley (Douglas)	68.46

1924 **6 September**

Scratch events in four classes with unlimited handicap.		
Over 600cc		
1st	S. Woods (New Imperial)	57.54
2nd	R. Price (Coventry-Eagle)	46.39
600cc		
1st	J. Craig (Norton)	67.86
2nd	C.A.R. Shillington (Norton)	61.65
3rd	J. Maxwell (Norton)	60.44
350cc		
1st	F. Andrews (New Imperial)	59.54
2nd	W. Andrews (New Imperial)	57.01
3rd	T. Stuart (Cotton)	54.14
250cc		
1st	J.A. Porter (New Gerrard)	59.16
2nd	J.A. Forsythe (Diamond)	56.55
3rd	L.T. Cridland (JES)	51.62
Fastest Lap	S. Woods (New Imperial)	72.71
Unlimited Handicap		
1st	J. Craig (Norton)	/
2nd	J.A. Forsythe (Diamond)	/
3rd	J.A. Porter (New Gerrard)	/

1925 **5 September**

Over 600cc		
1st	S. Woods (New Imperial)	65.26
2nd	F.R. Marston (HM Special)	58.54
3rd	C.F. Edwards (Brough-Superior)	55.51
600cc		
1st	J. Craig (Norton)	72.04
2nd	J.W. Shaw (Norton)	70.72
3rd	A. Bennett (Norton)	66.13
350cc		
1st	J.G. Burney (Enfield)	65.60
2nd	C. Anderson (DOT)	59.23
3rd	J. Wade (AJS)	57.87
250cc		
1st	W.A. Colgan (Cotton)	57.48
2nd	G. Wallace (OK)	50.77
3rd	W.S. Thompson (Cotton)	49.89
Fastest Lap	A. Bennett (Norton)	76.32
Unlimited Handicap		
1st	J.W. Shaw (Norton)	/
2nd	J. Craig (Norton)	/
3rd	J.G. Burney (Enfield)	/

1926 4 September

Scratch events in four classes; 600cc class replaced by 500cc; Unlimited handicap abolished.		
Over 500cc		
1st 2nd 3rd	J. Craig (Norton) T.E. Oliver (Scott) P. Blamire (Norton)	64.31 63.95 63.79
500cc		
1st 2nd 3rd	G.W. Walker (Sunbeam) T. Spann (Sunbeam) S. Ollerhead (Rudge)	70.43 66.94 64.94
350cc		
1st 2nd 3rd	W.L. Handley (Rex-Acme) T. Stewart (Enfield) C.J.P. Dodson (Sunbeam)	68.89 64.22 63.81
250cc	Only 2 finishers	
1st 2nd	S.A. Crabtree (Crabtree-JAP) W.A. Colgan (Cotton)	60.44 59.76
Fastest Lap	G.W. Walker (Sunbeam)	75.00

1927 3 September

Over 500cc		
1st 2nd 3rd	A. de Gourley (Norton) R. Matthews (Brough-Superior) G. Brockerton (Zenith)	66.12 62.04 60.58
500cc		
1st 2nd 3rd	J.W. Shaw (Norton) F.A. Longman (Rudge-Whitworth) S. Woods (Norton)	74.15 73.83 73.77
350cc		
1st 2nd 3rd	C.J.P. Dodson (Sunbeam) C.W. Hough (AJS) C.W. Johnson (Cotton)	71.55 68.73 66.14
250cc		
1st 2nd 3rd	W.A. Colgan (Cotton) H.G. Tyrell-Smith (Rex-Acme) A.E. Taylor (Rex-Acme)	63.35 59.22 58.12
Fastest Lap	S. Woods (Norton)	78.26

1928 1 September

Over 500cc	Only 1 finisher	
1st	G. Brockerton (Zenith)	67.17
500cc		
1st 2nd 3rd	G.W. Walker (Rudge) C.J.P. Dodson (Sunbeam) H.G. Tyrell-Smith (Rudge)	80.08 79.95 78.08
350cc		
1st 2nd 3rd	F.A. Longman (Velocette) L.H. Davenport (AJS) J.W. Shaw (Norton)	74.31 72.42 71.03
250cc	Only 2 finishers	
1st 2nd	F.L. Taylor (OK Supreme) L.C. Crabtree (Excelsior)	65.41 64.79
Fastest Lap	C.J.P. Dodson (Sunbeam)	81.72

1929 7 September

Over 500cc class dropped; scratch events in three classes: 500cc, 350cc and 250cc.		
500cc		
1st 2nd 3rd	G.W. Walker (Rudge) P. Hunt (Norton) S. Woods (Norton)	80.63 79.45 79.16
Fastest Lap	G.W. Walker (Rudge)	82.36
350cc		
1st 2nd 3rd	L.H. Davenport (AJS) G.E. Rowley (AJS) B.G. Corry (Velocette)	76.23 74.65 73.65
Fastest Lap	J. Craig (Norton)	78.34
250cc		
1st 2nd 3rd	F.A. Longman (OK Supreme) L.C. Crabtree (Excelsior) G.E. Himing (Zenith)	67.21 64.99 63.84
Fastest Lap	F.A. Longman (OK Supreme)	69.49

1930 **6 September**

500cc		
1st 2nd 3rd	S. Woods (Norton) C.J.P. Dodson (Sunbeam) H.G. Tyrell-Smith (Rudge)	80.56 80.43 79.76
Fastest Lap	J.H. Simpson (Norton)	84.63
350cc		
1st 2nd 3rd	L.H. Davenport (AJS) G.E. Nott (Rudge) A.G. Mitchell (Velocette)	75.19 73.71 73.29
Fastest Lap	L.H. Davenport (AJS)	78.93
250cc		
1st 2nd 3rd	S. Gleave (SGS) C.W. Johnson (OK Supreme) C.E. Needham (Rex-Acme)	67.63 65.61 64.94
Fastest Lap	S.A. Crabtree (Excelsior-JAP)	72.28

1931 **5 September**

500cc		
1st 2nd 3rd	S. Woods (Norton) G.E. Nott (Rudge) P. Hunt (Norton)	86.43 85.86 84.92
Fastest Lap	S. Woods (Norton)	89.67
350cc		
1st 2nd 3rd	L.H. Davenport (Norton) J. Guthrie (Norton) P.J. Walls (Rudge)	79.43 79.27 78.65
Fastest Lap	J. Guthrie (Norton)	83.29
250cc		
1st 2nd 3rd	E. Mitchell (Rudge) C.W. Johnson (Rudge) C.H. Manders (Rudge)	72.63 72.25 69.56
Fastest Lap	E. Mitchell (Rudge)	76.16

1932 **3 September**

500cc		
1st 2nd 3rd	S. Woods (Norton) P. Hunt (Norton) E.A. Simcock (Rudge)	85.15 84.18 82.90
Fastest Lap	S. Woods (Norton)	87.65
350cc		
1st 2nd 3rd	H.G. Tyrell-Smith (Rudge) C.H. Manders (Rudge) H. Pinnington (AJS)	77.89 76.75 71.43
Fastest Lap	J. Guthrie (Norton)	84.54
250cc		
1st 2nd 3rd	E.A. Mellors (New Imperial) S. Gleave (New Imperial) H. Pilling (CTS)	73.34 72.08 64.46
Fastest Lap	E.A. Mellors (New Imperial)	76.32

1933 **19 August**

500cc		
1st 2nd 3rd	S. Woods (Norton) W.F. Rusk (Norton) G.E. Nott (Rudge)	87.43 87.16 82.69
Fastest Lap	S. Woods (Norton) & P. Hunt (Norton)	89.56
350cc		
1st 2nd 3rd	W.L. Handley (Velocette) J. Guthrie (Norton) H.G. Tyrell-Smith (Velocette)	83.63 82.78 82.25
Fastest Lap	W.L. Handley (Velocette)	85.91
250cc		
1st 2nd 3rd	C.J.P. Dodson (New Imperial) C.H. Manders (Rudge) C. Taylor (CTS)	76.53 76.22 74.45
Fastest Lap	C. Manders (Rudge)	78.26

1934 **18 August**

500cc		
1st 2nd 3rd	W.F. Rusk (Velocette) C.J.P. Dodson (Norton) H.G. Tyrell-Smith (Rudge)	88.38 87.55 85.26
Fastest Lap	W.F. Rusk (Velocette)	92.13
350cc		
1st 2nd 3rd	J.H. Simpson (Norton) H.E. Newman (Velocette) W.H. Hey (Rudge)	84.93 84.90 79.19
Fastest Lap	H.E. Newman (Velocette)	86.82
250cc		
1st 2nd 3rd	G.E. Nott (Rudge) L.G. Martin (Cotton) S.V. Smith (New Imperial)	77.08 71.90 58.06
Fastest Lap	G.E. Nott (Rudge)	78.84

1935 **24 August**

Run in conjunction with Grand Prix D'Europe		
500cc		
1st 2nd 3rd	J. Guthrie (Norton) R. Milhoux (F.N.) A. Tyler (Velocette)	90.98 89.11 87.69
Fastest Lap	J. Guthrie (Norton)	95.35
350cc		
1st 2nd 3rd	W.L. Handley (Velocette) E.R. Thomas (Velocette) J.G. Duncan (Norton)	86.65 85.30 84.98
Fastest Lap	W.L. Handley (Velocette)	88.28
250cc		
1st 2nd 3rd	A. Geiss (DKW) A.R. Foster (New Imperial) J.G. Burney (Moto Guzzi)	79.16 79.03 77.48
Fastest Lap	A. Geiss (DKW)	83.20

1936 **22 August**

500cc		
1st 2nd 3rd	F.L. Frith (Norton) J.W. Beevers (Norton) W.G. Wright (Norton)	92.00 82.46 81.14
Fastest Lap	F.L. Frith (Norton)	95.23
350cc		
1st 2nd 3rd	E.R. Thomas (Velocette) E.A. Mellors (Velocette) J. Chambers (Norton)	86.82 86.18 83.65
Fastest Lap	J.H. White (Norton)	92.13
250cc		
1st 2nd 3rd	S. 'Ginger' Wood (New Imperial) A.R. Foster (New Imperial) C.H. Manders (Excelsior)	78.76 78.76 77.39
Fastest Lap	A.R. Foster (New Imperial)	80.83

1937 **21 August**

500cc		
1st 2nd 3rd	J.M. West (BMW) J. Moore (Norton) H. Taggart (AJS)	91.64 84.54 79.29
Fastest Lap	J.M. West (BMW)	93.65
350cc		
1st 2nd 3rd	E.A. Mellors (Velocette) A.R. Foster (AJS) G.E. Rowley (AJS)	85.58 84.99 84.64
Fastest Lap	E.A. Mellors (Velocette)	87.10
250cc		
1st 2nd 3rd	E.R. Thomas (DKW) S. 'Ginger' Wood (Excelsior) L.J. Archer (New Imperial)	81.83 80.65 76.80
Fastest Lap	E.R. Thomas (DKW)	83.96

1938 **20 August**

500cc		
1st	J.M. West (BMW)	93.98
2nd	S. 'Ginger' Wood (Velocette)	92.05
3rd	M.D. Whitworth (Velocette)	90.97
Fastest Lap	J.M. West (BMW)	98.93
350cc		
1st	E.A. Mellors (Velocette)	87.85
2nd	W.F. Rusk (Norton)	87.63
3rd	L.J. Archer (Velocette)	86.21
Fastest Lap	E.A. Mellors (Velocette)	90.89
250cc		
1st	E.R. Thomas (DKW)	80.48
2nd	H.G. Tyrell-Smith (Excelsior)	79.77
3rd	C. Tattersall (CTS)	74.70
Fastest Lap	E.R. Thomas (DKW)	84.44

1939 **19 August**

500cc		
1st	D. Serafini (Gilera)	97.85
2nd	F.L. Frith (Norton)	96.83
3rd	L.J. Archer (Velocette)	92.95
Fastest Lap	D. Serafini (Gilera)	100.03
350cc		
1st	S. Woods (Velocette)	91.65
2nd	H. Fleishmann (DKW)	89.28
3rd	S. Wünsche (DKW)	88.92
Fastest Lap	E.A. Mellors (Velocette)	93.54
250cc		
1st	L.G. Martin (Excelsior)	76.08
2nd	G. McAdam (Excelsior)	75.79
3rd	C. Tattersall (CTS)	74.62
Fastest Lap	L.G. Martin (Excelsior)	80.47

1947–52 inclusive, races held on the new modified Clady circuit (16.5 miles to the lap)

1947 **16 August**

500cc		
1st	A.J. Bell (Norton)	91.25
2nd	E. Lyons (Norton)	91.10
3rd	J.M. West (AJS)	90.43
Fastest Lap	A.J. Bell (Norton)	94.79
350cc		
1st	J. Lockett (Norton)	84.77
2nd	L.A. Dear (Velocette)	83.97
3rd	B.J. Goodman (Velocette)	81.66
Fastest Lap	J. Lockett (Norton)	86.51
250cc		
1st	M. Cann (Moto Guzzi)	78.78
2nd	M. Barrington (Moto Guzzi)	76.94
3rd	L.G. Martin (Excelsior)	74.20
Fastest Lap	M. Cann (Moto Guzzi)	81.08

1948 **21 August**

Run in conjunction with Grand Prix D'Europe.		
500cc		
1st	E. Lorenzetti (Moto Guzzi)	85.55
2nd	J. Lockett (Norton)	85.39
3rd	R.L. Graham (AJS)	82.67
Fastest Lap	E. Lorenzetti (Moto Guzzi)	88.57
350cc		
1st	F.L. Frith (Velocette)	80.16
2nd	K. Bills (Velocette)	79.58
3rd	F.W. Fry (Velocette)	79.37
Fastest Lap	F.L. Frith (Velocette)	81.86
250cc		
1st	M. Cann (Moto Guzzi)	72.47
2nd	J. McCredie (Excelsior)	65.52
3rd	H. Kirby (Excelsior)	64.13
Fastest Lap	M. Cann (Moto Guzzi)	74.29

1949 **20 August**

500cc		
1st 2nd 3rd	R.L. Graham (AJS) A.J. Bell (Norton) N. Pagani (Gilera)	96.49 95.47 95.37
Fastest Lap	R.L. Graham (AJS)	98.08
350cc		
1st 2nd 3rd	F.L. Frith (Velocette) C.F. Salt (Velocette) H.R. Armstrong (AJS)	89.12 88.80 88.72
Fastest Lap	F.L. Frith (Velocette)	90.60
250cc		
1st 2nd 3rd	M. Cann (Moto Guzzi) B. Ruffo (Moto Guzzi) R.A. Mead (Norton)	80.08 78.95 76.63
Fastest Lap	M. Cann (Moto Guzzi)	82.43

1950 **19 August**

500cc		
1st 2nd 3rd	G.E. Duke (Norton) R.L. Graham (AJS) J. Lockett (Norton)	99.56 98.92 98.46
Fastest Lap	G.E. Duke (Norton)	101.77
350cc		
1st 2nd 3rd	A.R. Foster (Velocette) H.R. Armstrong (Velocette) H. Hinton (Norton)	91.38 91.24 90.57
Fastest Lap	A.R. Foster (Velocette)	92.87
250cc		
1st 2nd 3rd	M. Cann (Moto Guzzi) D. Ambrosini (Benelli) W. Billington (Moto Guzzi)	82.73 78.29 77.64
Fastest Lap	M. Cann (Moto Guzzi)	84.18
125cc	Only 2 finishers	
1st 2nd	C. Ubbiali (Mondial) B. Ruffo (Mondial)	77.46 76.81
Fastest Lap	C. Ubbiali (Mondial)	78.92

1951 **16 & 18 August**

500cc		
1st 2nd 3rd	G.E. Duke (Norton) K. Kavanagh (Norton) U. Masetti (Gilera)	95.18 93.49 93.14
Fastest Lap	A. Milani (Gilera)	97.27
350cc		
1st 2nd 3rd	G.E. Duke (Norton) K. Kavanagh (Norton) J. Lockett (Norton)	96.85 95.21 95.21
Fastest Lap	G.E. Duke (Norton)	98.40
250cc		
1st 2nd 3rd	B. Ruffo (Moto Guzzi) M. Cann (Moto Guzzi) A.F. Wheeler (Velocette)	86.93 86.78 83.00
Fastest Lap	B. Ruffo (Moto Guzzi)	89.37
125cc		
1st 2nd 3rd	W.A.C. McCandless (Mondial) G. Zanzi (Mondial) C. Clegg (Anelay-Excelsior)	73.15 67.44 8 laps only
Fastest Lap	W.A.C. McCandless (Mondial)	76.19

1952 **14 & 16 August**

500cc		
1st 2nd 3rd	W.A.C. McCandless (Gilera) R.W. Coleman (AJS) W.A. Lomas (MV)	99.79 97.95 96.47
Fastest Lap	R.L. Graham (MV)	105.94
350cc		
1st 2nd 3rd	K. Kavanagh (Norton) H.R. Armstrong (Norton) R.W. Coleman (AJS)	94.88 93.93 92.80
Fastest Lap	K. Kavanagh (Norton)	97.11
250cc		
1st 2nd 3rd	M. Cann (Moto Guzzi) E. Lorenzetti (Moto Guzzi) R.L. Graham (Velocette)	86.22 85.88 84.21
Fastest Lap	E. Lorenzetti (Moto Guzzi)	88.97

125cc		
1st 2nd 3rd	C.C. Sandford (MV) W.A. Lomas (MV) C.F. Salt (MV)	77.47 76.33 10 laps only
Fastest Lap	C.C. Sandford (MV)	78.61

1953–64 inclusive, races held on the Dundrod circuit (7.415 miles to the lap)

1953 13 & 15 August

500cc		
1st 2nd 3rd	K. Kavanagh (Norton) G.E. Duke (Gilera) J. Brett (Norton)	89.81 89.28 88.96
Fastest Lap	G.E. Duke (Gilera) & K. Kavanagh (Norton)	91.74
350cc		
1st 2nd 3rd	K.H. Mudford (Norton) R. McIntyre (AJS) R.W. Coleman (AJS)	84.01 83.56 82.71
Fastest Lap	K.H. Mudford (Norton)	88.11
250cc		
1st 2nd 3rd	H.R. Armstrong (NSU) W. Haas (NSU) F.K. Anderson (Moto Guzzi)	81.76 81.54 80.11
Fastest Lap	H.R. Armstrong (NSU)	83.95
125cc		
1st 2nd 3rd	W. Haas (NSU) C.C. Sandford (MV) H.R. Armstrong (NSU)	74.87 74.39 74.38
Fastest Lap	W. Haas (NSU)	76.06
Sidecar		
1st 2nd 3rd	C. Smith (Norton) P.V. Harris (Norton) J. Drion (Norton)	77.79 75.25 71.15
Fastest Lap	E.S. Oliver (Norton)	79.17

1954 24 & 26 June

500cc		
1st 2nd 3rd	W.R. Amm (Norton) R.W. Coleman (AJS) G. Laing (Norton)	83.87 83.22 83.13
Fastest Lap	W.R. Amm (Norton)	85.02
350cc		
1st 2nd 3rd	W.R. Amm (Norton) J. Brett (Norton) R. McIntyre (AJS)	83.47 83.12 82.98
Fastest Lap	W.R. Amm (Norton)	88.70
250cc		
1st 2nd 3rd	W. Haas (NSU) H. Baltisberger (NSU) H.P. Müller (NSU)	77.62 77.61 75.83
Fastest Lap	W. Haas (NSU), R. Hollaus (NSU) & H. Baltisberger (NSU)	80.41
125cc		
1st 2nd 3rd	R. Hollaus (NSU) H.P. Müller (NSU) H. Baltisberger (NSU)	77.01 76.47 75.86
Fastest Lap	C. Ubbiali (MV)	79.22
Sidecar		
1st 2nd 3rd	E.S. Oliver (Norton) C. Smith (Norton) W. Noll (BMW)	76.49 75.88 74.69
Fastest Lap	E.S. Oliver (Norton)	78.38

1955 11 & 13 August

500cc		
1st 2nd 3rd	W.A. Lomas (Moto Guzzi) J. Hartle (Norton) R.H. Dale (Moto Guzzi)	92.30 92.22 89.88
Fastest Lap	W.A. Lomas (Moto Guzzi)	94.34
350cc		
1st 2nd 3rd	W.A. Lomas (Moto Guzzi) J. Hartle (Norton) J. Surtees (Norton)	89.31 89.11 88.24

Fastest Lap	W.A. Lomas (Moto Guzzi)	90.81
250cc		
1st 2nd 3rd	J. Surtees (NSU) S.H. Miller (NSU) U. Masetti (MV)	87.63 87.10 85.97
Fastest Lap	J. Surtees (NSU)	88.99

1956 **9 & 11 August**

500cc		
1st 2nd 3rd	J. Hartle (Norton) R.N. Brown (Matchless) G.A. Murphy (Matchless)	85.66 83.99 83.98
Fastest Lap	G.E. Duke (Gilera)	94.47
350cc		
1st 2nd 3rd	W.A. Lomas (Moto Guzzi) R.H. Dale (Moto Guzzi) J. Hartle (Norton)	90.26 89.61 89.39
Fastest Lap	W.A. Lomas (Moto Guzzi)	91.74
250cc		
1st 2nd 3rd	L. Taveri (MV) S.H. Miller (NSU) A.F. Wheeler (Moto Guzzi)	86.28 85.99 81.98
Fastest Lap	C. Ubbiali (MV)	89.41
125cc		
1st 2nd 3rd	C. Ubbiali (MV) R. Ferri (Gilera) W.M. Webster (MV)	81.00 79.21 66.26
Fastest Lap	C. Ubbiali (MV)	82.40
Sidecar		
1st 2nd 3rd	W. Noll (BMW) P.V. Harris (Norton) F. Camathias (BMW)	78.89 77.49 77.17
Fastest Lap	W. Noll (BMW)	81.15

1957 **10 August**

500cc		
1st 2nd 3rd	L. Liberati (Gilera) R. McIntyre (Gilera) G.E. Duke (Gilera)	91.56 90.98 90.64
Fastest Lap	J. Surtees (MV)	95.69
350cc		
1st 2nd 3rd	K.R. Campbell (Moto Guzzi) K. Bryen (Moto Guzzi) L. Liberati (Gilera)	85.28 84.93 81.88
Fastest Lap	K. Bryen (Moto Guzzi)	87.82
250cc		
1st 2nd 3rd	C.C. Sandford (Mondial) D.V. Chadwick (MV) T.H. Robb (NSU)	83.30 82.02 80.51
Fastest Lap	D.V. Chadwick (MV)	85.57
125cc		
1st 2nd 3rd	L. Taveri (MV) T. Provini (Mondial) R. Venturi (MV)	78.45 78.43 78.36
Fastest Lap	T. Provini (Mondial)	80.90

1958 **9 August**

500cc		
1st 2nd 3rd	J. Surtees (MV) R. McIntyre (Norton) J. Hartle (MV)	86.73 85.27 84.50
Fastest Lap	J. Surtees (MV)	89.53
350cc		
1st 2nd 3rd	J. Surtees (MV) J. Hartle (MV) T. Shepherd (Norton)	80.46 79.69 78.89
Fastest Lap	J. Surtees (MV) & J. Hartle (MV)	83.59
250cc		
1st 2nd 3rd	T. Provini (MV) T.H. Robb (NSU) D.V. Chadwick (MV)	77.41 75.55 74.48
Fastest Lap	T. Provini (MV)	80.71

125cc		
1st 2nd 3rd	C. Ubbiali (MV) L. Taveri (Ducati) D.V. Chadwick (Ducati)	77.04 75.86 75.59
Fastest Lap	A. Gandossi (Ducati)	79.03

1959 **8 August**

500cc		
1st 2nd 3rd	J. Surtees (MV) R. McIntyre (Norton) G.E. Duke (Norton)	95.28 94.79 92.61
Fastest Lap	J. Surtees (MV)	96.73
350cc		
1st 2nd 3rd	J. Surtees (MV) R.N. Brown (Norton) G.E. Duke (Norton)	91.32 89.30 89.29
Fastest Lap	J. Hartle (MV)	93.35
250cc		
1st 2nd 3rd	G. Hocking (MZ) S.M.B. Hailwood (Mondial) E. Degner (MZ)	89.26 88.62 87.01
Fastest Lap	G. Hocking (MZ)	91.12
125cc		
1st 2nd 3rd	S.M.B. Hailwood (Ducati) G. Hocking (MZ) E. Degner (MZ)	81.92 81.49 80.73
Fastest Lap	S.M.B. Hailwood (Ducati)	84.75

1960 **6 August**

500cc		
1st 2nd 3rd	J. Hartle (Norton) J. Surtees (MV) A. Shepherd (Matchless)	93.37 93.03 91.82
Fastest Lap	J. Surtees (MV)	99.32
350cc		
1st 2nd 3rd	J. Surtees (MV) J. Hartle (Norton) H.R. Anderson (AJS)	93.39 92.83 90.06
Fastest Lap	A. Shepherd (AJS)	95.42
250cc		
1st 2nd 3rd	C. Ubbiali (MV) T. Phillis (Honda) J. Redman (Honda)	90.83 90.78 90.73
Fastest Lap	C. Ubbiali (MV)	93.61
125cc		
1st 2nd 3rd	C. Ubbiali (MV) G. Hocking (MV) E. Degner (MZ)	83.38 83.33 83.16
Fastest Lap	E. Degner (MZ)	85.68

1961 **12 August**

500cc		
1st 2nd 3rd	G. Hocking (MV) S.M.B. Hailwood (Norton) A. King (Norton)	90.49 88.78 88.76
Fastest Lap	G. Hocking (MV)	98.37
350cc		
1st 2nd 3rd	G. Hocking (MV) A. King (Bianchi) F. Šťastný (Jawa)	92.90 92.30 91.15
Fastest Lap	G. Hocking (MV)	95.55
250cc		
1st 2nd 3rd	R. McIntyre (Honda) S.M.B. Hailwood (Honda) J. Redman (Honda)	95.44 94.98 94.10
Fastest Lap	R. McIntyre (Honda)	96.94
125cc		
1st 2nd 3rd	K. Takahashi (Honda) E. Degner (MZ) T. Phillis (Honda)	87.51 87.48 87.45
Fastest Lap	T. Phillis (Honda)	88.93

1962 11 August

500cc		
1st 2nd 3rd	S.M.B. Hailwood (MV) A. Shepherd (Matchless) P.W. Read (Norton)	96.55 92.14 91.05
Fastest Lap	S.M.B. Hailwood (MV)	99.99
350cc		
1st 2nd 3rd	J. Redman (Honda) F. Šťastný (Jawa) T.H. Robb (Honda)	93.76 92.25 92.00
Fastest Lap	S.M.B. Hailwood (MV)	95.08
250cc		
1st 2nd 3rd	T.H. Robb (Honda) J. Redman (Honda) L. Taveri (Honda)	88.39 86.66 86.65
Fastest Lap	L. Taveri (Honda)	91.06
125cc		
1st 2nd 3rd	L. Taveri (Honda) T.H. Robb (Honda) J. Redman (Honda)	83.30 83.30 83.29
Fastest Lap	T.H. Robb (Honda)	84.70

1963 10 August

500cc		
1st 2nd 3rd	S.M.B. Hailwood (MV) J. Hartle (Gilera) D.W. Minter (Gilera)	99.27 98.38 96.65
Fastest Lap	S.M.B. Hailwood (MV)	101.28
350cc		
1st 2nd 3rd	J. Redman (Honda) S.M.B. Hailwood (MV) L. Taveri (Honda)	93.78 93.22 91.73
Fastest Lap	J. Redman (Honda)	95.83
250cc		
1st 2nd 3rd	J. Redman (Honda) T. Provini (Morini) T.H. Robb (Honda)	86.64 86.48 85.98
Fastest Lap	T. Provini (Morini)	89.23
125cc		
1st 2nd 3rd	H.R. Anderson (Suzuki) B. Schneider (Suzuki) L. Taveri (Honda)	85.84 84.12 84.11
Fastest Lap	B. Schneider (Suzuki)	87.99

1964 8 August

500cc		
1st 2nd 3rd	P.W. Read (Norton) R. Creith (Norton) J.J. Ahearn (Norton)	82.24 82.21 81.75
Fastest Lap	P.W. Read (Norton)	84.17
350cc		
1st 2nd 3rd	J. Redman (Honda) M.A. Duff (AJS) G. Havel (Jawa)	93.82 91.12 90.60
Fastest Lap	J. Redman (Honda)	96.10
250cc		
1st 2nd 3rd	P.W. Read (Yamaha) J. Redman (Honda) R. Bryans (Honda)	85.91 84.75 83.86
Fastest Lap	P.W. Read (Yamaha)	87.42
125cc		
1st 2nd 3rd	H.R. Anderson (Suzuki) L. Taveri (Honda) R. Bryans (Honda)	91.53 90.29 90.15
Fastest Lap	H.R. Anderson (Suzuki)	93.67

1965–present, races held on the new modified Dundrod circuit (7.401 miles to the lap)

1965 7 August

500cc		
1st 2nd 3rd	R. Creith (Norton) E.G. Driver (Matchless) C.R. Conn (Norton)	86.20 86.04 86.03
Fastest Lap	E.G. Driver (Matchless)	91.49

350cc		
1st 2nd 3rd	F. Šťastný (Jawa) B. Beale (Honda) G. Havel (Jawa)	91.01 90.39 88.67
Fastest Lap	J. Redman (Honda)	99.54
250cc		
1st 2nd 3rd	P.W. Read (Yamaha) M.A. Duff (Yamaha) D. Woodman (MZ)	86.04 85.36 84.67
Fastest Lap	P.W. Read (Yamaha)	87.88
125cc		
1st 2nd 3rd	E. Degner (Suzuki) K. Enderlein (MZ) D. Woodman (MZ)	86.41 82.31 81.74
Fastest Lap	E. Degner (Suzuki)	90.81

1966 **20 August**

500cc		
1st 2nd 3rd	S.M.B. Hailwood (Honda) G. Agostini (MV) F. Šťastný (Jawa)	102.44 100.14 94.99
Fastest Lap	S.M.B. Hailwood (Honda)	105.03
350cc		
1st 2nd 3rd	S.M.B. Hailwood (Honda) G. Agostini (MV) T.H. Robb (Bultaco)	95.50 93.69 86.80
Fastest Lap	S.M.B. Hailwood (Honda)	97.21
250cc		
1st 2nd 3rd	W.G. Molloy (Bultaco) G. Marsovszky (Bultaco) K.C. Cass (Bultaco)	87.03 86.09 85.37
Fastest Lap	P.W. Read (Yamaha)	92.81
125cc		
1st 2nd 3rd	L. Taveri (Honda) R. Bryans (Honda) P.W. Read (Yamaha)	92.38 92.25 91.56
Fastest Lap	R. Bryans (Honda)	94.45

1967 **19 August**

500cc		
1st 2nd 3rd	S.M.B. Hailwood (Honda) J. Hartle (Matchless) J. Findlay (Matchless)	102.88 99.20 98.06
Fastest Lap	S.M.B. Hailwood (Honda)	106.71
350cc		
1st 2nd 3rd	G. Agostini (MV) R. Bryans (Honda) H. Rosner (MZ)	103.31 103.05 14 laps only
Fastest Lap	G. Agostini (MV)	105.11
250cc		
1st 2nd 3rd	S.M.B. Hailwood (Honda) R. Bryans (Honda) W.D. Ivy (Yamaha)	104.31 103.55 103.20
Fastest Lap	S.M.B. Hailwood (Honda)	105.86
125cc		
1st 2nd 3rd	W.D. Ivy (Yamaha) P.W. Read (Yamaha) S. Graham (Suzuki)	94.81 94.81 91.36
Fastest Lap	W.D. Ivy (Yamaha)	99.53

1968 **17 August**

500cc		
1st 2nd 3rd	G. Agostini (MV) R. Fitton (Norton) J. Hartle (Matchless-Metisse)	94.89 90.57 90.38
Fastest Lap	G. Agostini (MV)	97.57
350cc		
1st 2nd 3rd	G. Agostini (MV) K. Carruthers (Aermacchi-Metisse) B. Steenson (Aermacchi)	102.74 96.23 95.74
Fastest Lap	G. Agostini (MV)	106.37
250cc		
1st 2nd 3rd	W.D. Ivy (Yamaha) H. Rosner (MZ) R. Gould (Yamaha)	97.50 94.45 93.26
Fastest Lap	W.D. Ivy (Yamaha)	103.64

125cc		
1st 2nd 3rd	W.D. Ivy (Yamaha) P.W. Read (Yamaha) H. Rosner (MZ)	99.65 99.54 10 laps only
Fastest Lap	P.W. Read (Yamaha)	102.44

1969 **16 August**

500cc		
1st 2nd 3rd	G. Agostini (MV) B. Steenson (Seeley) M. Uphill (Norton)	103.74 98.60 95.94
Fastest Lap	G. Agostini (MV)	107.66
350cc		
1st 2nd 3rd	G. Agostini (MV) H. Rosner (MZ) C. Crawford (Aermacchi)	99.01 95.64 95.01
Fastest Lap	G. Agostini (MV)	102.60
250cc		
1st 2nd 3rd	K. Carruthers (Benelli) K. Andersson (Yamaha) R. McCullough (Yamaha)	93.61 90.96 90.81
Fastest Lap	K. Carruthers (Benelli)	98.87
50cc		
1st 2nd 3rd	Á. Nieto (Derbi) J. De Vries (Kreidler) F. Whiteway (Suzuki)	80.20 77.75 69.58
Fastest Lap	P. Lodewijkx (Jamathi)	83.39
Sidecar		
1st 2nd 3rd	K. Enders (BMW) S. Schauzu (BMW) F.D. Linnarz (BMW)	88.94 87.34 86.80
Fastest Lap	K. Enders (BMW)	90.79

1970 **15 August**

500cc		
1st 2nd 3rd	G. Agostini (MV) W.G. Molloy (Kawasaki) P.H. Tait (Seeley)	101.88 98.91 98.07
Fastest Lap	G. Agostini (MV)	107.14
350cc		
1st 2nd 3rd	G. Agostini (MV) G. Bartusch (MZ) T.H. Robb (Yamaha)	102.61 99.75 99.44
Fastest Lap	G. Agostini (MV)	105.03
250cc		
1st 2nd 3rd	K. Carruthers (Yamaha) R. Gould (Yamaha) P. Smart (Yamaha)	100.03 99.12 96.84
Fastest Lap	K. Carruthers (Yamaha)	101.89
50cc		
1st 2nd 3rd	Á. Nieto (Derbi) S. Canellas (Derbi) A. Toersen (Jamathi)	82.40 81.30 81.27
Fastest Lap	Á. Nieto (Derbi)	83.95
Sidecar		
1st 2nd 3rd	K. Enders (BMW) S. Schauzu (BMW) J.C. Castella (BMW)	85.82 84.31 83.13
Fastest Lap	K. Enders (BMW)	92.17

1971 **14 August**

500cc		
1st 2nd 3rd	J. Findlay (Suzuki) R. Bron (Suzuki) T.H. Robb (Seeley)	95.01 93.69 93.05
Fastest Lap	J. Findlay (Suzuki)	97.00
350cc		
1st 2nd 3rd	P.J. Williams (MZ) D. Braun (Yamaha) T. Jefferies (Yamaha)	88.31 87.44 87.16
Fastest Lap	J. Saarinen (Yamaha)	92.17

250cc		
1st 2nd 3rd	R. McCullough (Yamsel) J. Saarinen (Yamaha) D. Braun (Yamaha)	92.74 90.78 90.54
Fastest Lap	R. McCullough (Yamsel)	94.83
Sidecar		
1st 2nd 3rd	H. Owesle (Munch) S. Schauzu (BMW) H. Luthringshauser (BMW)	91.13 90.94 90.42
Fastest Lap	H. Owesle (Munch)	92.23

1972 **UGP cancelled due to NI political unrest.**

1973 **18 August**

500cc		
1st 2nd 3rd	J.G. Williams (Yamaha) W. Guthrie (Yamaha) D. Chatterton (Yamaha)	104.26 100.49 100.35
Fastest Lap	J.G. Williams (Yamaha)	105.69
350cc		
1st 2nd 3rd	J.G. Williams (Yamaha) T.Rutter (Yamaha) C.I. Williams (Yamaha)	103.72 103.71 102.57
Fastest Lap	T. Rutter (Yamaha)	107.06
250cc		
1st 2nd 3rd	J.G. Williams (Yamaha) R. McCullough (Yamsel) C.I. Williams (Yamaha)	100.39 100.23 100.14
Fastest Lap	J.G. Williams (Yamaha)	102.84
Sidecar		
1st 2nd 3rd	D. Keen (Konig) W.E. Cooper (WEC) B. Moran (Norton)	87.77 86.77 86.68
Fastest Lap	D. Keen (Konig) & B. Crook (Windle)	89.56

1974 **17 August**

500cc		
1st 2nd 3rd	T. Rutter (Yamaha) D. Chatterton (Yamaha) P. McKinley (Yamaha)	104.75 104.52 103.05
Fastest Lap	T. Rutter (Yamaha)	106.03
350cc		
1st 2nd 3rd	T. Rutter (Yamaha) A. Alexander (Yamaha) D. Chatterton (Yamaha)	104.07 103.41 102.68
Fastest Lap	T. Rutter (Yamaha)	106.62
250cc		
1st 2nd 3rd	A.R. Hockley (Yamaha) P. McKinley (Yamaha) D. Chatterton (Yamaha)	100.57 100.24 99.99
Fastest Lap	R. McCullough (Yamaha)	103.64
200cc		
1st 2nd 3rd	C. Junk (Honda) R. Garnett (Honda) N. Tuxworth (Yamaha)	89.53 88.11 88.08
Fastest Lap	C. Junk (Honda)	90.84
Sidecar		
1st 2nd 3rd	D. Edgington (Windle-Konig) B. Moran (Norton) A. Lewis (Triumph)	91.58 86.86 86.73
Fastest Lap	P.J. Williams (KGB Imp)	95.16

1975 **16 August**

1000cc		
1st 2nd 3rd	P.H. Tait (Yamaha) R. Marshall (Yamaha) T. Herron (Yamaha)	106.97 105.17 104.29
Fastest Lap	P.H. Tait (Yamaha)	107.96
500cc		
1st 2nd 3rd	M. Robinson (Yamsel) T. Rutter (Yamaha) G.M.R. Barry (Yamsel)	98.18 97.91 96.69
Fastest Lap	T. Rutter (Yamaha)	106.66

350cc		
1st 2nd 3rd	R. McCullough (Yamaha) T. Herron (Yamaha) A. George (Yamaha)	106.85 105.36 104.88
Fastest Lap	R. McCullough (Yamaha)	108.57
250cc		
1st 2nd 3rd	T. Rutter (Yamaha) T. Herron (Yamaha) J. Weeden (Yamaha)	102.34 101.76 101.19
Fastest Lap	T. Rutter (Yamaha)	104.08
200cc		
1st 2nd 3rd	C. Junk (Honda) R.D. McQuillan (Rotax) W.S. McKee (Honda)	88.75 * *
Fastest Lap	C. Junk (Honda)	90.14

1976 **21 August**

1000cc		
1st 2nd 3rd	G.M.R. Barry (Yamaha) T. Rutter (Yamaha) S. Woods (Suzuki)	112.17 111.76 111.27
Fastest Lap	G.M.R. Barry (Yamaha)	114.55
500cc		
1st 2nd 3rd	S. Woods (Suzuki) J. Dunlop (Yamsel) T. Rutter (Yamaha)	109.46 108.79 108.68
Fastest Lap	S. Woods (Suzuki)	111.30
350cc		
1st 2nd 3rd	R. McCullough (Yamaha) I. Richards (Yamaha) J. Weeden (Yamaha)	108.63 107.62 107.37
Fastest Lap	R. McCullough (Yamaha)	110.56
250cc		
1st 2nd 3rd	R. McCullough (Yamaha) T. Rutter (Yamaha) I. Richards (Yamaha)	105.19 104.66 104.34
Fastest Lap	R. McCullough (Yamaha)	107.18

* information unavailable

200cc		
1st 2nd 3rd	N. Tuxworth (Yamaha) R.I. Nesbitt (Yamaha) J.R. Hanna (Suzuki)	91.19 * *
Fastest Lap	N. Tuxworth (Yamaha)	93.23

1977 **20 August**

1000cc		
1st 2nd 3rd	J.G. Williams (Yamaha) T. Rutter (Yamaha) D. Potter (Yamaha)	114.97 114.70 112.64
Fastest Lap	J.G. Williams (Yamaha)	117.48
500cc		
1st 2nd 3rd	J.G. Williams (Suzuki) B. Smith (Suzuki) J. Woodley (Suzuki)	113.41 109.65 109.56
Fastest Lap	J.G. Williams (Suzuki)	115.04
350cc		
1st 2nd 3rd	T. Herron (Yamaha) R. McCullough (Yamaha) J. Ekerold (Yamaha)	111.16 111.07 111.02
Fastest Lap	R. McCullough (Yamaha)	113.86
250cc		
1st 2nd 3rd	T. Herron (Yamaha) A. North (Yamaha) P. Nurmi (Yamaha)	108.14 108.14 106.85
Fastest Lap	T. Herron (Yamaha)	110.65
Sidecar		
1st 2nd 3rd	M. Boddice (Yamaha) G. Brodin (Yamaha) B. Hodgkins (Yamaha)	102.62 102.61 101.01
Fastest Lap	J. Taylor (Yamaha)	105.06

1978 12 August

1000cc		
1st 2nd 3rd	T. Herron (Yamaha) T. Rutter (Yamaha) R. Marshall (Yamaha)	116.71 115.24 114.39
Fastest Lap	T. Herron (Yamaha)	118.84
500cc		
1st 2nd 3rd	J.G. Williams (Suzuki) T. Herron (Suzuki) J. Woodley (Suzuki)	111.95 111.14 110.47
Fastest Lap	T. Herron (Suzuki)	115.74
350cc		
1st 2nd 3rd	J. Ekerold (Yamaha) G. Waring (Yamaha) S. Tonkin (Yamaha)	111.44 110.44 110.16
Fastest Lap	J. Ekerold (Yamaha)	113.19
250cc		
1st 2nd 3rd	T. Herron (Yamaha) J. Ekerold (Yamaha) T. Steele (Yamaha)	107.50 106.75 106.52
Fastest Lap	T. Herron (Yamaha)	109.56
TT Formula 1		
1st 2nd 3rd	T. Herron (Honda) T. Rutter (Honda) J. Cowie (Kawasaki)	110.46 109.65 109.19
Fastest Lap	T. Herron (Honda)	113.96
Sidecar		
1st 2nd 3rd	M. Boddice (Yamaha) D. Saville (Yamaha) P. Coney (Yamaha)	102.52 101.40 100.22
Fastest Lap	M. Boddice (Yamaha)	105.73

500cc		
1st 2nd 3rd	J. Dunlop (Suzuki) J. Newbold (Suzuki) D. Ireland (Suzuki)	112.76 112.36 112.05
Fastest Lap	J. Dunlop (Suzuki)	115.54
350cc		
1st 2nd 3rd	D. Robinson (Yamaha) J. Dunlop (Yamaha) B. Jackson (Yamaha)	110.73 109.93 109.88
Fastest Lap	B. Jackson (Yamaha)	112.23
250cc		
1st 2nd 3rd	R. McCullough (Yamaha) B. Jackson (Yamaha) G. McGregor (Yamaha)	107.61 107.61 107.21
Fastest Lap	R. McCullough (Yamaha)	109.47
TT Formula 1		
1st 2nd 3rd	R. Haslam (Honda) T. Rutter (Honda) G. Crosby (Kawasaki)	112.90 112.00 110.95
Fastest Lap	R. Haslam (Honda)	116.15
TT Formula 2		
1st 2nd 3rd	A. Jackson (Honda) D. Mason (Honda) R. Bowler (Honda)	99.70 98.06 95.85
Fastest Lap	A. Jackson (Honda)	100.39
TT Formula 3		
1st 2nd 3rd	B. Smith (Yamaha) W.A. Smith (Honda) L. Trotter (Honda)	94.90 93.70 92.80
Fastest Lap	B. Smith (Yamaha)	96.19

1979 18 August

1000cc		
1st 2nd 3rd	J. Dunlop (Yamaha) R. Marshall (Yamaha) J. Newbold (Yamaha)	115.34 115.33 113.43
Fastest Lap	J. Dunlop (Yamaha)	117.58

1980 16 August

1000cc		
1st 2nd 3rd	J. Dunlop (Suzuki) R. Marshall (Yamaha) J. Newbold (Suzuki)	116.39 116.23 116.21
Fastest Lap	J. Dunlop (Suzuki)	118.95

500cc		
1st 2nd 3rd	D. Robinson (Suzuki) D. Ireland (Suzuki) J. Woodley (Suzuki)	111.83 110.88 110.77
Fastest Lap	S. Cull (Suzuki)	114.55
350cc		
1st 2nd 3rd	R. McCullough (Yamaha) D. Robinson (Yamaha) T. Rutter (Yamaha)	109.58 109.57 108.31
Fastest Lap	R. McCullough (Yamaha)	110.83
250cc		
1st 2nd 3rd	J. Dunlop (Yamaha) D. Robinson (Yamaha) R. McCullough (Yamaha)	107.71 107.39 107.38
Fastest Lap	J. Dunlop (Yamaha)	109.20
TT Formula 1		
1st 2nd 3rd	G. Crosby (Suzuki) J. Dunlop (Suzuki) M. Grant (Honda)	114.32 114.31 113.38
Fastest Lap	J. Dunlop (Suzuki)	117.27
TT Formula 2		
1st 2nd 3rd	C.I. Williams (Yamaha) M. Lucas (Honda) N. Hudson (Honda)	100.68 99.97 98.46
Fastest Lap	M. Lucas (Honda)	101.77
TT Formula 3		
1st 2nd 3rd	R. Haslam (Honda) D. Casement (Yamaha) R. Hunter (Suzuki)	96.70 95.13 93.16
Fastest Lap	R. Haslam (Honda)	98.68

1981 **22 August**

Superbike		
1st 2nd 3rd	R. Haslam (Honda) M. Grant (Suzuki) J. Newbold (Suzuki)	108.54 108.00 107.02
Fastest Lap	R. Haslam (Honda)	111.11

500cc		
1st 2nd 3rd	G. Lingham (Suzuki) J. Newbold (Suzuki) C.I. Williams (Yamaha)	101.50 101.36 100.89
Fastest Lap	J. Newbold (Suzuki)	104.90
350cc		
1st 2nd 3rd	G. McGregor (Yamaha) R. McCullough (Yamaha) D. Huxley (Yamaha)	102.77 102.26 102.09
Fastest Lap	D. Robinson (Yamaha)	104.98
250cc		
1st 2nd 3rd	T. Rutter (Yamaha) C. Junk (Yamaha) D. Chatterton (Yamaha)	95.90 95.77 95.66
Fastest Lap	S. Cull (Yamaha) & P. Mellor (Yamaha)	99.64
TT Formula 1		
1st 2nd 3rd	R. Haslam (Honda) G. Crosby (Suzuki) M. Grant (Suzuki)	105.95 104.96 104.64
Fastest Lap	R. Haslam (Honda)	107.61
TT Formula 2		
1st 2nd 3rd	P. Mellor (Yamaha) T. Rutter (Ducati) P. Odlin (Honda)	96.89 96.18 93.38
Fastest Lap	P. Mellor (Yamaha)	99.05
TT Formula 3		
1st 2nd 3rd	B. Smith (Yamaha) D. Casement (Yamaha) W.A. Smith (Honda)	86.65 86.00 85.60
Fastest Lap	J. Millar (Aermacchi)	88.46

1982 **21 August**

Superbike		
1st 2nd 3rd	R. Marshall (Suzuki) J. Dunlop (Honda) R. Haslam (Honda)	118.30 118.03 116.56
Fastest Lap	R. Marshall (Suzuki)	119.91

500cc		
1st 2nd 3rd	P. Cranston (Yamaha) S. McClements (Suzuki) C. Law (Yamaha)	107.29 102.52 102.19
Fastest Lap	P. Cranston (Yamaha)	110.28
350cc		
1st 2nd 3rd	R. McCullough (Yamaha) P. Mellor (Yamaha) R. McElnea (Yamaha)	110.30 110.17 109.97
Fastest Lap	P. Mellor (Yamaha) & R. McElnea (Yamaha)	111.95
250cc		
1st 2nd 3rd	D. Robinson (Yamaha) B. Reid (Yamaha) S. Tonkin (Armstrong)	104.34 103.07 102.82
Fastest Lap	D. Robinson (Yamaha)	105.81
TT Formula 1		
1st 2nd 3rd	R. Haslam (Honda) J. Dunlop (Honda) W. Gardner (Honda)	116.72 115.40 112.76
Fastest Lap	N. Brown (Suzuki)	118.10
TT Formula 2		
1st 2nd 3rd	T. Rutter (Ducati) D. Robinson (Yamaha) G. Fogarty (Ducati)	100.73 100.67 97.04
Fastest Lap	T. Rutter (Ducati)	104.40

1983 **20 August**

500cc		
1st 2nd 3rd	R. Marshall (Honda) B. Reid (Suzuki) J. Dunlop (Honda)	110.86 109.11 108.03
Fastest Lap	B. Reid (Suzuki)	113.09
350cc		
1st 2nd 3rd	B. Reid (Yamaha) J. Rea (Yamaha) P. Mellor (Yamaha)	97.76 95.76 95.21
Fastest Lap	B. Reid (Yamaha)	105.48
250cc		
1st 2nd 3rd	B. Reid (Yamaha) T. Rutter (Yamaha) M. Barr (Yamaha)	98.69 98.17 97.72
Fastest Lap	B. Reid (Yamaha)	101.62
TT Formula 1		
1st 2nd 3rd	J. Dunlop (Honda) M. Grant (Suzuki) R. McElnea (Suzuki)	107.38 106.49 106.46
Fastest Lap	J. Dunlop (Honda)	110.10
TT Formula 2		
1st 2nd 3rd	P. Mellor (Yamaha) T. Rutter (Ducati) G. McGregor (Ducati)	110.16 109.98 108.73
Fastest Lap	T. Rutter (Ducati)	112.04

1984 **18 August**

500cc		
1st 2nd 3rd	J. Dunlop (Honda) M. Grant (Suzuki) R. Marshall (Honda)	118.17 118.02 118.00
Fastest Lap	J. Dunlop (Honda)	120.62
350cc		
1st 2nd 3rd	T. Steele (Yamaha) S. Cull (Yamaha) E. Roberts (Yamaha)	106.37 105.75 105.13
Fastest Lap	M. Farmer (Yamaha)	109.60
250cc		
1st 2nd 3rd	J. Dunlop (Honda) B. Reid (EMC) P. Tinker (Armstrong)	110.55 110.55 109.59
Fastest Lap	J. Dunlop (Honda)	113.04
TT Formula 1		
1st 2nd 3rd	J. Dunlop (Honda) R. Marshall (Honda) M. Grant (Suzuki)	114.28 114.18 112.31
Fastest Lap	J. Dunlop (Honda)	117.74

TT Formula 2		
1st 2nd 3rd	J. Weeden (Yamaha) D. Barry (Yamaha) T. Rutter (Ducati)	101.03 100.46 100.22
Fastest Lap	B. Reid (Yamaha)	104.08

1985 **17 August**

500cc		
1st 2nd 3rd	J. Dunlop (Honda) S. Cull (Suzuki) D. Ireland (Suzuki)	116.14 115.87 114.60
Fastest Lap	J. Dunlop (Honda)	119.16
350cc		
1st 2nd 3rd	S. Cull (Yamaha) G. Cowan (Yamaha) M. Farmer (Yamaha)	111.43 111.42 110.43
Fastest Lap	G. Cowan (Yamaha)	114.25
250cc		
1st 2nd 3rd	J. Dunlop (Honda) S. Cull (Honda) M. Farmer (EMC)	111.96 111.23 109.43
Fastest Lap	J. Dunlop (Honda)	114.21
TT Formula 1		
1st 2nd 3rd	J. Dunlop (Honda) M. Grant (Suzuki) G. McGregor (Suzuki)	114.45 112.45 112.18
Fastest Lap	J. Dunlop (Honda)	116.81
TT Formula 2		
1st 2nd 3rd	B. Reid (Yamaha) E. Laycock (Yamaha) N. Tuxworth (Yamaha)	111.19 111.14 107.99
Fastest Lap	B. Reid (Yamaha)	113.86

1986 **16 August**

Superbike		
1st 2nd 3rd	J. Dunlop (Honda) R. Marshall (Honda) A. McGladdery (Suzuki)	118.29 117.43 115.57
Fastest Lap	J. Dunlop (Honda)	120.83
Superstock		
1st 2nd 3rd	P. Mellor (Suzuki) A. McGladdery (Suzuki) K. Dobson (Honda)	111.60 111.30 111.25
Fastest Lap	A. McGladdery (Suzuki)	113.81
350cc		
1st 2nd 3rd	E. Laycock (Yamaha) G. Cowan (Yamaha) D. Todd (Yamaha)	111.51 109.90 109.71
Fastest Lap	E. Laycock (Yamaha)	112.37
250cc		
1st 2nd 3rd	S. Cull (Honda) I. Newton (Armstrong) M. Farmer (Honda)	102.60 101.15 101.00
Fastest Lap	S. Cull (Honda)	105.15
TT Formula 1		
1st 2nd 3rd	N. Robinson (Suzuki) J. Dunlop (Honda) A. McGladdery (Suzuki)	110.42 108.22 106.54
Fastest Lap	N. Robinson (Suzuki)	112.00
TT Formula 2		
1st 2nd 3rd	E. Laycock (Yamaha) B. Reid (Yamaha) S. Hislop (Yamaha)	105.27 102.82 101.52
Fastest Lap	E. Laycock (Yamaha)	107.18

1987 **15 August**

TT F1 race abandoned following a fatal accident; rest cancelled due to weather.		
350cc		
1st 2nd 3rd	B. Reid (Yamaha) G. Cowan (Honda) W. Coulter (Honda)	108.28 107.85 105.45
Fastest Lap	B. Reid (Yamaha)	109.87

1988 **30 July**

Superbike		
1st 2nd 3rd	E. Laycock (Honda) J. Dunlop (Honda) S. Hislop (Honda)	120.14 119.15 119.06
Fastest Lap	E. Laycock (Honda)	121.39
Superstock		
1st 2nd 3rd	N. Jefferies (Honda) D. Griffith (Honda) A. McGladdery (Suzuki)	101.66 101.46 101.20
Fastest Lap	S. Hislop (Honda)	105.27
350cc (A)		
1st 2nd 3rd	B. Reid (Yamaha) E. Laycock (EMC) W. Coulter (Honda)	109.09 108.96 107.64
Fastest Lap	E. Laycock (EMC)	111.48
350cc (B)		
1st 2nd 3rd	J. Dunlop (Honda) W. Coulter (Honda) S. Williams (Yamaha)	112.31 112.31 112.28
Fastest Lap	J. Dunlop (Honda)	114.21
TT Formula 1		
1st 2nd 3rd	C. Fogarty (Honda) S. Hislop (Honda) R. Dunlop (Honda)	111.01 110.39 109.88
Fastest Lap	C. Fogarty (Honda)	116.10

1989 **12 August**

Superbike		
1st 2nd 3rd	C. Fogarty (Honda) S. Hislop (Honda) E. Laycock (Honda)	120.50 119.86 119.81
Fastest Lap	C. Fogarty (Honda)	121.63
Supersport 600cc		
1st 2nd 3rd	B. Reid (Yamaha) P. McCallen (Honda) J. Whitham (Suzuki)	112.25 111.90 111.89
Fastest Lap	B. Reid (Yamaha)	113.09
Supersport 400cc		
1st 2nd 3rd	E. Laycock (Suzuki) J. Rea (Suzuki) I. Lougher (Suzuki)	108.95 107.59 107.02
Fastest Lap	E. Laycock (Suzuki)	110.14
350cc		
1st 2nd 3rd	E. Laycock (Yamaha) B. Reid (Yamaha) W. Coulter (Yamaha)	106.73 105.86 105.16
Fastest Lap	E. Laycock (Yamaha)	111.66
TT Formula 1		
1st 2nd 3rd	S. Hislop (Honda) C. Fogarty (Honda) S. Cull (Norton)	118.02 118.01 116.75
Fastest Lap	S. Hislop (Honda)	121.12
Sidecar		
1st 2nd 3rd	D. Brindley (Sabre) D. Saville (Sabre) J. Thompson (Yamaha)	98.81 98.69 97.14
Fastest Lap	D. Brindley (Sabre)	100.92

1990 **11 August**

Superbike		
1st 2nd 3rd	S. Hislop (Honda) R. Dunlop (Norton) E. Laycock (Honda)	121.46 121.24 121.23
Fastest Lap	S. Hislop (Honda)	123.72
Supersport 600cc		
1st 2nd 3rd	S. Cull (Yamaha) D. Leach (Yamaha) B. Reid (Yamaha)	113.42 113.41 113.36
Fastest Lap	D. Leach (Yamaha)	116.29
350cc		
1st 2nd 3rd	B. Reid (Yamaha) S. Hislop (Honda) J. Dunlop (Honda)	116.03 115.48 115.09
Fastest Lap	B. Reid (Yamaha)	117.36
TT Formula 1		
1st 2nd 3rd	J. Dunlop (Honda) R. Dunlop (Norton) D. Leach (Yamaha)	120.87 120.07 117.45
Fastest Lap	J. Dunlop (Honda)	122.94
125cc		
1st 2nd 3rd	R. Dunlop (Honda) J. Dunlop (Honda) A. Caughey (Honda)	104.78 104.75 104.74
Fastest Lap	A. Caughey (Honda)	106.14

1991 **10 August**

Superbike (A)		
1st 2nd 3rd	J. Dunlop (Honda) P. McCallen (Honda) R. Dunlop (Norton)	118.36 118.35 115.75
Fastest Lap	P. McCallen (Honda)	120.12
Superbike (B)		
1st 2nd 3rd	J. Dunlop (Honda) P. McCallen (Honda) R. Dunlop (Norton)	110.09 110.00 105.06
Fastest Lap	P. McCallen (Honda)	112.48
Supersport 600cc		
1st 2nd 3rd	J. Rea (Yamaha) P. McCallen (Honda) D. Leach (Yamaha)	114.44 114.10 113.93
Fastest Lap	J. Rea (Yamaha)	116.07
Supersport 400cc		
1st 2nd 3rd	P. McCallen (Honda) D. Leach (Yamaha) B. Reid (Honda)	107.88 107.46 106.35
Fastest Lap	P. McCallen (Honda)	108.85
350cc		
1st 2nd 3rd	P. McCallen (Honda) I. Lougher (Yamaha) D. Milling (Yamaha)	106.88 104.43 102.96
Fastest Lap	P. McCallen (Honda)	108.99
125cc		
1st 2nd 3rd	R. Dunlop (Honda) J. Dunlop (Honda) D. Lemon (Honda)	106.30 106.16 104.50
Fastest Lap	R. Dunlop (Honda)	108.30

1992 **20 June**

Superbike (A)		
1st 2nd 3rd	R. Dunlop (Norton) S. Ward (Honda) I. Duffus (Kawasaki)	115.56 114.91 114.90
Fastest Lap	R. Dunlop (Norton)	117.11
Superbike (B)		
1st 2nd 3rd	R. Dunlop (Norton) N. Jefferies (Honda) R. Holden (Yamaha)	116.84 116.70 115.42
Fastest Lap	R. Dunlop (Norton)	118.59
Supersport 600cc		
1st 2nd 3rd	I. Simpson (Honda) A. Irwin (Honda) B. Jackson (Honda)	111.38 111.36 111.32
Fastest Lap	A. Irwin (Honda)	112.69

Supersport 400cc		
1st 2nd 3rd	B. Reid (Yamaha) I. Duffus (Yamaha) N. Jefferies (Honda)	107.31 107.30 105.14
Fastest Lap	B. Reid (Yamaha) & I. Duffus (Yamaha)	109.08
350cc		
1st 2nd 3rd	B. Reid (Yamaha) R. Dunlop (Yamaha) D. Milling (Yamaha)	112.14 112.10 109.80
Fastest Lap	R. Dunlop (Yamaha)	113.66
125cc		
1st 2nd 3rd	J. Dunlop (Honda) M. Lofthouse (Honda) I. Lougher (Honda)	102.18 102.02 101.86
Fastest Lap	J. Courtney (Honda)	103.94

1993 **5 & 7 August**

Superbike		
1st 2nd 3rd	P. McCallen (Honda) J. Dunlop (Honda) N. Jefferies (Honda)	117.62 117.48 117.46
Fastest Lap	P. McCallen (Honda)	119.35
Supersport 600cc		
1st 2nd 3rd	P. McCallen (Honda) I. Simpson (Honda) B. Reid (Honda)	107.58 107.03 105.95
Fastest Lap	I. Simpson (Honda)	109.90
Supersport 400cc		
1st 2nd 3rd	I. Duffus (Yamaha) I. Simpson (Yamaha) A. Murphy (Yamaha)	108.04 108.03 106.31
Fastest Lap	I. Simpson (Yamaha)	109.44
350cc		
1st 2nd 3rd	P. McCallen (Honda) R. Dunlop (Yamaha) L. Pullan (Yamaha)	109.91 109.11 108.03
Fastest Lap	R. Dunlop (Yamaha)	114.16
125cc		
1st 2nd 3rd	R. Dunlop (Honda) M. Lofthouse (Honda) J. Dunlop (Honda)	105.66 105.65 105.63
Fastest Lap	M. Lofthouse (Honda)	107.43
Historic 1000cc (A)		
1st 2nd 3rd	A. Moyce (BSA) T. Reid (BSA) A. Donaldson (Weslake)	100.91 99.97 97.90
Fastest Lap	A. Moyce (BSA)	101.92
Historic 1000cc (B)		
1st 2nd 3rd	T. Reid (BSA) K. Harrison (Triumph) S. Parkhill (BSA)	102.69 102.53 101.19
Fastest Lap	K. Harrison (Triumph)	103.94
Historic 500cc (A)		
1st 2nd 3rd	B. Jackson (Matchless) J. O'Kane (Matchless) G. Bell (Matchless)	95.78 94.12 94.11
Fastest Lap	B. Jackson (Matchless)	96.87
Historic 500cc (B)		
1st 2nd 3rd	B. Jackson (Matchless) J. O'Kane (Matchless) J. Weeden (Matchless)	96.80 93.50 93.14
Fastest Lap	B. Jackson (Matchless)	97.56
Historic 350cc (A)		
1st 2nd 3rd	B. Swallow (Aermacchi) W. Seawright (Honda) M. Baldwin (Aermacchi)	92.43 88.68 87.69
Fastest Lap	B. Swallow (Aermacchi)	93.92
Historic 350cc (B)		
1st 2nd 3rd	G. Tunstall (Aermacchi) N. Jamison (Honda) M. Baldwin (Aermacchi)	89.26 87.66 86.40
Fastest Lap	G. Tunstall (Aermacchi)	91.34

1994 12 & 13 August

Superbike (A)		
1st 2nd 3rd	J. Dunlop (Honda) P. McCallen (Honda) J. Griffiths (Kawasaki)	123.23 123.22 123.15
Fastest Lap	P. McCallen (Honda)	125.03
Superbike (B)		
1st 2nd 3rd	P. McCallen (Honda) J. Griffiths (Kawasaki) A Irwin (Kawasaki)	124.38 124.37 121.33
Fastest Lap	J. Griffiths (Kawasaki)	126.10
Supersport 600cc		
1st 2nd 3rd	P. McCallen (Honda) I. Duffus (Yamaha) B. Gardiner (Honda)	116.59 116.24 113.66
Fastest Lap	P. McCallen (Honda)	119.00
Supermono		
1st 2nd 3rd	J. Griffiths (Yamaha) D. Morris (BMW) B. Jackson (MHD)	109.99 109.21 105.26
Fastest Lap	R. Holden (Ducati)	112.90
250cc (A)		
1st 2nd 3rd	P. McCallen (Honda) J. Courtney (Honda) J. Dunlop (Honda)	117.92 117.41 116.13
Fastest Lap	P. McCallen (Honda)	119.48
250cc (B)		
1st 2nd 3rd	P. McCallen (Honda) J. Dunlop (Honda) J. Courtney (Honda)	118.07 117.93 117.32
Fastest Lap	P. McCallen (Honda)	119.64
125cc		
1st 2nd 3rd	J. Dunlop (Honda) I. Lougher (Aprilia) P. Owens (Honda)	108.83 108.81 108.77
Fastest Lap	P. Owens (Honda) & M. Lofthouse (Yamaha)	110.24

Historic 1000cc		
1st 2nd 3rd	R. Holden (Triumph) D. Pither (Triumph) A. Donaldson (Weslake)	107.87 106.60 102.97
Fastest Lap	R. Holden (Triumph)	110.01
Historic 500cc		
1st 2nd 3rd	B. Jackson (Seeley) B. Swallow (Matchless) M. Robinson (Seeley)	101.51 100.99 99.15
Fastest Lap	B. Jackson (Seeley)	102.63
Historic 350cc		
1st 2nd 3rd	B. Swallow (Aermacchi) N. Jamison (Honda) G. Jamison (Honda)	96.60 93.71 92.40
Fastest Lap	B. Swallow (Aermacchi)	97.06
Historic 250cc		
1st 2nd 3rd	B. Jackson (Suzuki) A. Elwood (Suzuki) B. O'Kane (Yamaha)	98.43 78.13 77.25
Fastest Lap	B. Jackson (Suzuki)	100.20

1995 18 & 19 August

Superbike (A)		
1st 2nd 3rd	J. Dunlop (Honda) R. Holden (Ducati) N. Jefferies (Honda)	122.25 121.67 121.21
Fastest Lap	J. Dunlop (Honda)	124.54
Superbike (B)		
1st 2nd 3rd	R. Holden (Ducati) N. Jefferies (Honda) I. Duffus (Ducati)	122.12 122.11 121.45
Fastest Lap	N. Jefferies (Honda)	124.22
Supersport 600cc		
1st 2nd 3rd	I. Duffus (Honda) S. Ward (Honda) J. Griffiths (Kawasaki)	117.53 117.52 117.49
Fastest Lap	J. Griffiths (Kawasaki)	119.07

250cc (A)		
1st	J. Dunlop (Honda)	117.94
2nd	M. Lofthouse (Yamaha)	117.64
3rd	J. Courtney (Honda)	117.63
Fastest Lap	J. Dunlop (Honda)	119.51

250cc (B)		
1st	J. Dunlop (Honda)	118.25
2nd	J. Courtney (Honda)	117.84
3rd	J. Griffiths (Yamaha)	117.73
Fastest Lap	J. Dunlop (Honda)	119.64

125cc		
1st	J. Courtney (Honda)	109.78
2nd	P. Owens (Honda)	109.39
3rd	M. Lofthouse (Yamaha)	109.36
Fastest Lap	J. Courtney (Honda)	110.52

Sidecar (Open)		
1st	D. Molyneux (Krauser)	107.42
2nd	A. Budge (Suzuki)	106.82
3rd	C. O'Neill (Kawasaki)	104.85
Fastest Lap	A. Budge (Suzuki)	109.44

Sidecar (F2)		
1st	R. Fisher (Yamaha)	107.94
2nd	G. Bell (Yamaha)	105.52
3rd	M. Boddice (Honda)	105.48
Fastest Lap	R. Fisher (Yamaha)	108.69

Historic 1000cc		
1st	R. Holden (Triumph)	107.95
2nd	A. Walsh (Triumph)	101.95
3rd	C. Bevan (BSA)	101.62
Fastest Lap	R. Holden (Triumph)	109.56

Historic 500cc		
1st	J. Cronshaw (BSA)	102.66
2nd	B. Jackson (Matchless)	102.58
3rd	W. Seawright (Drixton)	99.58
Fastest Lap	J. Cronshaw (BSA)	105.11

Historic 350cc		
1st	N. McWhirter (Honda)	96.80
2nd	G. Heath (Honda)	96.15
3rd	D. Welsh (Honda)	96.09
Fastest Lap	N. McWhirter (Honda)	98.67

Historic 250cc		
1st	B. Jackson (Suzuki)	98.03
2nd	N. Dorman (Honda)	81.34
3rd	G. O'Kane (Honda)	80.71
Fastest Lap	B. Jackson (Suzuki)	99.41

1996 **1 & 3 August**

Superbike (A)		
1st	P. McCallen (Honda)	122.90
2nd	S. Beck (Kawasaki)	122.63
3rd	J. Griffiths (Honda)	122.32
Fastest Lap	P. McCallen (Honda)	124.00

Superbike (B)		
1st	P. McCallen (Honda)	123.36
2nd	B. Jackson (Kawasaki)	123.15
3rd	J. Griffiths (Honda)	123.15
Fastest Lap	P. McCallen (Honda)	124.98

Supersport 600cc		
1st	P. McCallen (Honda)	119.30
2nd	J. Griffiths (Honda)	118.65
3rd	B. Gardiner (Honda)	117.87
Fastest Lap	P. McCallen (Honda)	120.45

250cc (A)		
1st	P. McCallen (Honda)	117.78
2nd	P. Owens (Aprilia)	117.56
3rd	D. McCullough (Honda)	116.67
Fastest Lap	P. McCallen (Honda)	118.89

250cc (B)		
1st	P. McCallen (Honda)	117.37
2nd	A. Patterson (Yamaha)	116.92
3rd	D. Young (Honda)	116.92
Fastest Lap	D. Young (Honda)	118.42

125cc		
1st	P. Owens (Honda)	109.80
2nd	D. McCullough (Honda)	109.22
3rd	G. Dynes (Honda)	108.58
Fastest Lap	P. Owens (Honda)	111.03

Sidecar (Open)		
1st 2nd 3rd	R. Fisher (Suzuki) D. Hendry (Suzuki) C. O'Neill (Kawasaki)	109.48 105.71 105.47
Fastest Lap	R. Fisher (Suzuki)	110.65
Sidecar (F2)		
1st 2nd 3rd	K. Howles (Yamaha) V. Biggs (Yamaha) G. Lambert (Yamaha)	108.53 104.96 104.79
Fastest Lap	K. Howles (Yamaha)	110.68
Historic 1000cc		
1st 2nd 3rd	A. Walsh (Triumph) G. Wilson (Norton) K. Wilkie (Triumph)	100.06 99.34 97.55
Fastest Lap	A. Walsh (Triumph)	102.17
Historic 500cc		
1st 2nd 3rd	J. Cronshaw (BSA) N. Jefferies (Norton) G. English (Matchless)	103.69 103.68 103.65
Fastest Lap	N. Jefferies (Norton)	105.91
Historic 350cc		
1st 2nd 3rd	D. Welch (Honda) G. Jamison (Honda) C. Rodgers (Honda)	85.77 85.35 83.74
Fastest Lap	D. Welch (Honda)	87.75
Historic 250cc		
1st 2nd 3rd	B. Jackson (Suzuki) C. Dawson (Suzuki) G. Long (Suzuki)	86.56 84.21 80.01
Fastest Lap	B. Jackson (Suzuki)	88.65

1997 **23 August**

Superbike (A)		
1st 2nd 3rd	J. Griffiths (Honda) J. Courtney (Honda) J. Dunlop (Honda)	122.90 122.64 122.54
Fastest Lap	J. Griffiths (Honda)	124.63
Superbike (B)		
1st 2nd 3rd	S. Beck (Kawasaki) J. Griffiths (Honda) J. Courtney (Honda)	109.39 108.74 107.92
Fastest Lap	S. Beck (Kawasaki)	110.86
Supersport 600cc		
1st 2nd 3rd	B. Jackson (Honda) D. Young (Honda) J. Griffiths (Honda)	118.87 118.85 118.84
Fastest Lap	B. Jackson (Honda)	120.59
250cc (A)		
1st 2nd 3rd	O. McNally (Aprilia) J. Courtney (Honda) J. Dunlop (Honda)	116.97 116.50 116.29
Fastest Lap	D. Young (Honda)	118.49
250cc (B)		
1st 2nd 3rd	J. Dunlop (Honda) M. Fissette (Honda) R. Farquhar (Honda)	118.66 118.66 117.88
Fastest Lap	M. Fissette (Honda)	120.27
125cc		
1st 2nd 3rd	P. Owens (Honda) J. Dunlop (Honda) C. Richardson (Honda)	98.46 97.51 97.46
Fastest Lap	P. Owens (Honda)	100.01

1998 **20 & 22 August**

Superbike (A)		
1st 2nd 3rd	J. Griffiths (Honda) M. Rutter (Honda) S. Beck (Kawasaki)	114.65 114.43 113.78
Fastest Lap	J. Griffiths (Honda)	118.15
Superbike (B)		
1st 2nd 3rd	I. Simpson (Honda) J. Courtney (Honda) J. Griffiths (Honda)	123.23 123.22 123.17
Fastest Lap	I. Simpson (Honda)	125.03

Supersport 600cc		
1st 2nd 3rd	J. Griffiths (Honda) I. Simpson (Honda) R. Britton (Honda)	116.61 116.25 115.68
Fastest Lap	J. Griffiths (Honda)	119.07
250cc (A)		
1st 2nd 3rd	I. Lougher (Honda) J. Creith (Honda) O. McNally (Aprilia)	114.47 113.98 113.97
Fastest Lap	J. Creith (Honda)	115.96
250cc (B)		
1st 2nd 3rd	O. McNally (Aprilia) I. Lougher (Honda) G. Dynes (Honda)	118.62 118.62 116.87
Fastest Lap	I. Lougher (Honda)	120.24
125cc		
1st 2nd 3rd	R. Dunlop (Honda) P. Owens (Honda) I. Lougher (Honda)	109.82 109.47 109.47
Fastest Lap	R. Dunlop (Honda)	111.03
Historic 1000cc		
1st 2nd 3rd	C. Bevan (Weslake Metisse) K. Wilkie (Triumph) R. Kennedy (Triton)	98.57 96.59 89.94
Fastest Lap	C. Bevan (Weslake Metisse)	99.37
Historic 500cc		
1st 2nd 3rd	B. Swallow (Norton) G. Bell (Seeley) A. Moyce (Honda)	101.46 97.48 97.28
Fastest Lap	B. Swallow (Norton)	102.41
Historic 350cc		
1st 2nd 3rd	B. Swallow (Aermacchi) C. Rodgers (Honda) G. Bell (Seeley)	91.61 91.60 86.89
Fastest Lap	C. Rodgers (Honda)	93.88

Historic 250cc		
1st 2nd 3rd	C. Junk (Suzuki) C Dawson (Suzuki) C. Blair (Suzuki)	86.37 85.51 80.76
Fastest Lap	C. Dawson (Suzuki)	87.95

1999 **19 & 21 August**

Superbike (A)		
1st 2nd 3rd	D. Jefferies (Yamaha) I. Duffus (Yamaha) J. Dunlop (Honda)	124.69 124.67 124.65
Fastest Lap	I. Lougher (Honda)	125.58
Superbike (B)		
1st 2nd 3rd	J. Dunlop (Honda) D. Jefferies (Yamaha) I. Duffus (Yamaha)	125.14 124.95 124.87
Fastest Lap	D. Jefferies (Yamaha)	126.86
Supersport 600cc		
1st 2nd 3rd	I. Duffus (Yamaha) D. Jefferies (Yamaha) J. Griffiths (Yamaha)	119.61 119.60 119.58
Fastest Lap	A. Archibald (Honda)	120.83
250cc (A)		
1st 2nd 3rd	A. Patterson (Honda) I. Lougher (Honda) J. Creith (Honda)	119.66 119.65 119.62
Fastest Lap	A. Patterson (Honda)	120.89
250cc (B)		
1st 2nd 3rd	O. McNally (Aprilia) A. Patterson (Honda) I. Lougher (Honda)	119.37 119.20 119.18
Fastest Lap	O. McNally (Aprilia)	120.76
125cc		
1st 2nd 3rd	P. Owens (Honda) J. Dunlop (Honda) I. Lougher (Honda)	111.17 111.16 111.15
Fastest Lap	G. Dynes (Honda)	112.47

Historic 1000cc	Only 2 finishers	
1st 2nd	D. Gallagher (Weslake) J. Jones (BSA)	105.46 100.76
Fastest Lap	D. Gallagher (Weslake)	107.62
Historic 500cc		
1st 2nd 3rd	W. Seawright (Drixton) A. Moyce (Drixton) G. Bell (Seeley)	101.43 101.28 97.73
Fastest Lap	B. Swallow (Norton)	105.33
Historic 350cc		
1st 2nd 3rd	B. Swallow (Aermacchi) J. Bell (Seeley) G. Jamison (Honda)	98.85 94.36 93.83
Fastest Lap	B. Swallow (Aermacchi)	99.83
Historic 250cc		
1st 2nd 3rd	Y. Holland (Suzuki) T. Ferguson (Honda) R. Wright (Honda)	91.34 75.92 75.76
Fastest Lap	C. Dawson (Suzuki)	92.10

2000 **19 August**

Superbike (A)		
1st 2nd 3rd	D. Jefferies (Yamaha) J. Griffiths (Yamaha) A. Archibald (Honda)	124.52 124.43 124.42
Fastest Lap	J. Griffiths (Yamaha)	125.46
Superbike (B)		
1st 2nd 3rd	D. Jefferies (Yamaha) J. Griffiths (Yamaha) I. Lougher (Yamaha)	125.61 125.31 123.73
Fastest Lap	D. Jefferies (Yamaha)	126.70
Supersport 600cc		
1st 2nd 3rd	I. Lougher (Yamaha) A. Archibald (Honda) J. Griffiths (Yamaha)	121.04 120.98 120.92
Fastest Lap	A. Archibald (Honda)	122.40
125cc		
1st 2nd 3rd	R. Dunlop (Honda) D. Lemon (Honda) J. Crumpton (Honda)	108.63 107.49 107.36
Fastest Lap	R. Dunlop (Honda)	109.71
Production 1000cc		
1st 2nd 3rd	A. Archibald (Honda) R. Britton (Yamaha) I. Duffus (Honda)	121.15 120.05 119.96
Fastest Lap	A. Archibald (Honda)	122.44
Historic 1000cc		
1st 2nd 3rd	D. Gallagher (Weslake) G. Sawyer (BSA) C. Adie (BSA)	102.67 97.47 84.85
Fastest Lap	D. Gallagher (Weslake)	104.07
Historic 500cc		
1st 2nd 3rd	B. Swallow (Norton) A. Moyce (Drixton) S. Linsdell (Seeley)	101.02 98.46 97.50
Fastest Lap	B. Swallow (Norton)	102.25
Historic 350cc		
1st 2nd 3rd	T. Keys (Yamaha) C. Rodgers (Honda) B. Swallow (Aermacchi)	98.27 97.03 96.65
Fastest Lap	T. Keys (Yamaha)	98.80
Historic 250cc		
1st 2nd 3rd	P. Thorne (Yamaha) S. Crompton (Yamaha) T. Kavanagh (Ducati)	85.23 83.04 75.65
Fastest Lap	N. Moore (Suzuki)	93.92

2001 **18 August**

Superbike (A)		
1st 2nd 3rd	I. Lougher (Suzuki) D. Jefferies (Yamaha) A. Archibald (Honda)	124.18 124.01 123.34
Fastest Lap	I. Lougher (Suzuki)	124.92

Superbike (B)		
1st 2nd 3rd	A. Archibald (Honda) D. Jefferies (Yamaha) R. Farquhar (Yamaha)	110.88 109.68 108.12
Fastest Lap	A. Archibald (Honda)	112.59
Supersport 600cc		
1st 2nd 3rd	A. Archibald (Honda) D. Jefferies (Yamaha) R. Britton (Yamaha)	119.50 119.26 118.72
Fastest Lap	R. Britton (Yamaha)	120.50
125cc		
1st 2nd 3rd	R. Dunlop (Honda) I. Lougher (Honda) J. Crumpton (Honda)	108.44 108.43 106.76
Fastest Lap	R. Dunlop (Honda)	109.54
Production 1000cc		
1st 2nd 3rd	I. Lougher (Suzuki) I. Duffus (Suzuki) A. McFarland (Suzuki)	123.36 123.14 122.60
Fastest Lap	I. Lougher (Suzuki)	124.33
National 1000cc		
1st 2nd 3rd	R. Quayle (Honda) G. Jess (Yamaha) B. Anstey (Yamaha)	119.68 119.60 119.54
Fastest Lap	B. Anstey (Yamaha)	121.33
Historic 350cc		
1st 2nd 3rd	C. Rodgers (Honda) P. Sharp (Aermacchi) T. Myers (Aermacchi)	89.37 87.65 87.00
Fastest Lap	C. Rodgers (Honda)	89.61
Historic 250cc		
1st 2nd 3rd	A. 'Bud' Jackson (Suzuki) T. Ferguson (Suzuki) P. Wakefield (Suzuki)	85.86 80.73 80.39
Fastest Lap	G. McMullan (Suzuki)	87.03

2002 17 August

Superbike (A)		
1st 2nd 3rd	I. Lougher (Suzuki) R. Britton (Suzuki) A. Archibald (Suzuki)	126.49 125.88 125.87
Fastest Lap	I. Lougher (Suzuki)	127.82
Superbike (B)		
1st 2nd 3rd	I. Lougher (Suzuki) R. Britton (Suzuki) B. Anstey (Suzuki)	126.17 125.25 124.70
Fastest Lap	I. Lougher (Suzuki)	127.60
Supersport 600cc		
1st 2nd 3rd	I. Lougher (Suzuki) I. Duffus (Suzuki) D. Lindsay (Suzuki)	120.68 120.65 120.11
Fastest Lap	I. Lougher (Suzuki)	122.11
Supersport 400cc		
1st 2nd 3rd	R. Farquhar (Kawasaki) G. Jess (Kawasaki) B. Gardiner (Kawasaki)	108.61 108.45 108.37
Fastest Lap	B. Gardiner (Kawasaki)	111.05
250cc		
1st 2nd 3rd	D. Lindsay (Honda) D. Burns (Honda) R. McCready (Honda)	113.05 111.57 109.21
Fastest Lap	D. Lindsay (Honda)	117.99
125cc		
1st 2nd 3rd	D. Lindsay (Honda) J. Crumpton (Honda) I. Lougher (Honda)	107.01 106.01 105.99
Fastest Lap	D. Lindsay (Honda)	110.08
Production 1000cc		
1st 2nd 3rd	D. Jefferies (Suzuki) A. Archibald (Suzuki) I. Lougher (Suzuki)	124.73 123.97 123.27
Fastest Lap	A. Archibald (Suzuki)	126.34

Production 600cc		
1st 2nd 3rd	D. Lindsay (Suzuki) G. Jess (Yamaha) J. Donnan (Yamaha)	118.99 118.67 115.80
Fastest Lap	D. Lindsay (Honda)	120.78
Historic 1000cc		
1st 2nd 3rd	G. Jamison (Weslake) W. Seawright (Triumph) B. Wark (Honda)	98.20 96.86 95.28
Fastest Lap	G. Jamison (Weslake)	99.23

2003 **16 August**

Superbike (A)		
1st 2nd 3rd	A. Archibald (Suzuki) R. Farquhar (Suzuki) I. Lougher (Suzuki)	126.96 126.90 126.55
Fastest Lap	A. Archibald (Suzuki)	128.20
Superbike (B)		
1st 2nd 3rd	I. Lougher (Suzuki) B. Anstey (Suzuki) R. Britton (Suzuki)	126.37 126.36 125.79
Fastest Lap	A. Archibald (Suzuki)	128.10
Supersport 600cc		
1st 2nd 3rd	I. Lougher (Honda) A. Archibald (Suzuki) R. Farquhar (Kawasaki)	122.13 122.12 122.10
Fastest Lap	A. Archibald (Suzuki)	123.40
Supersport 400cc		
1st 2nd 3rd	I. Duffus (Kawasaki) R. Farquhar (Kawasaki) J. Griffiths (Yamaha)	109.90 109.89 109.80
Fastest Lap	J. Griffiths (Yamaha)	111.74
125cc		
1st 2nd 3rd	R. Dunlop (Honda) I. Lougher (Honda) D. Lemon (Honda)	110.59 110.58 110.52
Fastest Lap	I. Lougher (Honda)	111.95

Production 1000cc		
1st 2nd 3rd	B. Anstey (Suzuki) A. Archibald (Suzuki) R. Farquhar (Suzuki)	126.35 126.34 125.49
Fastest Lap	B. Anstey (Suzuki)	127.95
Production 600cc		
1st 2nd 3rd	D. Lindsay (Yamaha) I. Lougher (Honda) J. McGuinness (Yamaha)	120.91 120.85 120.66
Fastest Lap	D. Lindsay (Yamaha)	122.59
Forgotten Era		
1st 2nd 3rd	T. Keys (Yamaha) D. Young (Yamaha) D. Hedison (Yamaha)	106.82 106.80 100.26
Fastest Lap	T. Keys (Yamaha)	108.48

2004 **21 August**

Superbike		
1st 2nd 3rd	B. Anstey (Suzuki) J. McGuinness (Kawasaki) R. Farquhar (Kawasaki)	127.60 127.59 126.59
Fastest Lap	B. Anstey (Suzuki)	129.03
Supersport 600cc		
1st 2nd 3rd	B. Anstey (Suzuki) R. Farquhar (Kawasaki) R. Britton (Honda)	122.37 122.36 122.32
Fastest Lap	B. Anstey (Suzuki)	124.10
Supersport 400cc		
1st 2nd 3rd	A. Buxton (Kawasaki) J. Phillips (Kawasaki) D. Bailie (Kawasaki)	104.19 104.18 101.91
Fastest Lap	J. Phillips (Kawasaki)	106.03
125cc		
1st 2nd 3rd	C. Palmer (Honda) I. Lougher (Honda) R. Dunlop (Honda)	109.00 108.99 108.87
Fastest Lap	C. Palmer (Honda)	110.96

Production 1000cc		
1st 2nd 3rd	R. Farquhar (Kawasaki) A. Archibald (Suzuki) J. Griffiths (Yamaha)	124.84 124.48 123.07
Fastest Lap	R. Farquhar (Kawasaki)	126.92
Production 600cc		
1st 2nd 3rd	B. Anstey (Suzuki) R. Farquhar (Kawasaki) J. McGuinness (Yamaha)	119.85 119.79 119.75
Fastest Lap	J. McGuinness (Yamaha)	122.27

2005 — 13 August

Superbike (A)		
1st 2nd 3rd	I. Lougher (Honda) B. Anstey (Suzuki) R. Farquhar (Honda)	120.67 120.55 119.41
Fastest Lap	G. Martin (Suzuki)	128.16
Superbike (B)		
1st 2nd 3rd	I. Lougher (Honda) G. Martin (Suzuki) R. Britton (Honda)	119.00 118.90 118.88
Fastest Lap	R. Britton (Honda)	123.20
Superstock		
1st 2nd 3rd	I. Lougher (Honda) A. Archibald (Suzuki) G. Martin (Suzuki)	124.02 122.98 122.96
Fastest Lap	I. Lougher (Honda)	125.55
Supersport 600cc (A)		
1st 2nd 3rd	J. McGuinness (Honda) A. Archibald (Suzuki) B. Anstey (Suzuki)	122.76 122.75 122.26
Fastest Lap	A. Archibald (Suzuki)	123.97
Supersport 600cc (B)		
1st 2nd 3rd	R. Farquhar (Kawasaki) M. Finnegan (Honda) C. Donald (Honda)	114.86 114.46 114.10
Fastest Lap	C. Donald (Honda)	117.16

250cc		
1st 2nd 3rd	J. McGuinness (Honda) W. Dunlop (Yamaha) N. Rank (Honda)	115.56 114.74 114.64
Fastest Lap	J. McGuinness (Honda)	117.87

2006 — 19 August

Superbike (A)		
1st 2nd 3rd	G. Martin (Yamaha) R. Porter (Honda) I. Lougher (Honda)	129.16 129.14 128.81
Fastest Lap	G. Martin (Yamaha)	130.54
Superbike (B)		
1st 2nd 3rd	G. Martin (Yamaha) I. Lougher (Honda) I. Hutchinson (Kawasaki)	128.75 128.45 128.43
Fastest Lap	I. Hutchinson (Kawasaki)	130.83
Superstock		
1st 2nd 3rd	B. Anstey (Suzuki) G. Martin (Yamaha) D. Lindsay (Suzuki)	121.91 121.68 120.63
Fastest Lap	B. Anstey (Suzuki)	125.76
Supersport 600cc (A)		
1st 2nd 3rd	G. Martin (Yamaha) I. Hutchinson (Kawasaki) I. Lougher (Honda)	123.78 123.74 122.93
Fastest Lap	I. Hutchinson (Kawasaki)	125.26
Supersport 600cc (B)		
1st 2nd 3rd	G. Martin (Yamaha) I. Hutchinson (Kawasaki) I. Lougher (Honda)	123.77 123.76 123.54
Fastest Lap	I. Hutchinson (Kawasaki)	125.43
250cc		
1st 2nd 3rd	D. Lindsay (Honda) I. Lougher (Honda) W. Dunlop (Honda)	120.12 120.05 119.88
Fastest Lap	D. Lindsay (Honda)	121.86

2007 **18 August**

Superbike		
1st 2nd 3rd	I. Hutchinson (Honda) G. Martin (Honda) B. Anstey (Suzuki)	117.25 116.26 115.14
Fastest Lap	I. Hutchinson (Honda)	118.98
Superstock		
1st 2nd 3rd	R. Farquhar (Kawasaki) C. Cummins (Yamaha) R. Frost (Yamaha)	117.30 115.10 113.42
Fastest Lap	R. Farquhar (Kawasaki)	118.90
Supersport 600cc		
1st 2nd 3rd	G. Martin (Honda) C. Cummins (Yamaha) R. Farquhar (Kawasaki)	115.74 115.59 115.13
Fastest Lap	G. Martin (Honda)	119.15
250cc		
1st 2nd 3rd	W. Dunlop (Honda) M. Dunlop (Honda) D. Burns (Honda)	109.86 109.73 109.69
Fastest Lap	W. Dunlop (Honda)	112.45

2008 **14 August**

Saturday's races cancelled due to weather		
125cc		
1st 2nd 3rd	I. Lougher (Honda) W. Dunlop (Honda) M. Dunlop (Honda)	108.83 108.82 106.25
Fastest Lap	W. Dunlop (Honda)	109.88

2009 **13 & 15 August**

Superbike (A)		
1st 2nd 3rd	C. Cummins (Kawasaki) I. Hutchinson (Honda) G. Martin (Honda)	131.37 131.36 131.26
Fastest Lap	I. Hutchinson (Honda)	133.23
Superbike (B)		
1st 2nd 3rd	G. Martin (Honda) G. Johnson (Honda) I. Hutchinson (Honda)	131.14 131.13 131.12
Fastest Lap	G. Johnson (Honda)	132.43
Superstock		
1st 2nd 3rd	I. Hutchinson (Honda) R. Farquhar (Kawasaki) K. Amor (Honda)	125.33 125.29 124.05
Fastest Lap	I. Hutchinson (Honda)	130.11
Supersport 600cc (A)		
1st 2nd 3rd	R. Farquhar (Kawasaki) I. Hutchinson (Honda) W. Dunlop (Yamaha)	125.16 125.16 125.10
Fastest Lap	I. Hutchinson (Honda)	126.96
Supersport 600cc (B)		
1st 2nd 3rd	W. Dunlop (Yamaha) R. Farquhar (Kawasaki) B. Anstey (Suzuki)	125.79 125.39 125.31
Fastest Lap	W. Dunlop (Yamaha)	127.58
Supertwins		
1st 2nd 3rd	R. Farquhar (Kawasaki) L. Hill (Suzuki) C. Gibson (Suzuki)	111.16 108.35 108.23
Fastest Lap	R. Farquhar (Kawasaki)	112.16
250cc		
1st 2nd 3rd	W. Dunlop (Honda) M. Dunlop (Honda) P. Owen (Honda)	118.83 118.67 113.92
Fastest Lap	W. Dunlop (Honda)	121.11
125cc		
1st 2nd 3rd	I. Lougher (Honda) M. Dunlop (Honda) C. Elkin (Honda)	110.72 107.49 106.25
Fastest Lap	W. Dunlop (Honda)	113.37

2010 12 & 14 August

Superbike (A)		
1st 2nd 3rd	I. Hutchinson (Honda) B. Anstey (Suzuki) K. Amor (BMW)	131.58 131.57 131.54
Fastest Lap	K. Amor (BMW)	133.21
Superbike (B)		
1st 2nd 3rd	B. Anstey (Suzuki) I. Hutchinson (Honda) K. Amor (BMW)	132.03 132.02 131.98
Fastest Lap	B. Anstey (Suzuki)	133.97
Superstock		
1st 2nd 3rd	I. Hutchinson (Honda) K. Amor (BMW) R. Farquhar (Kawasaki)	130.20 130.17 129.08
Fastest Lap	I. Hutchinson (Honda)	132.16
Supersport 600cc (A)		
1st 2nd 3rd	I. Hutchinson (Honda) K. Amor (Honda) M. Dunlop (Yamaha)	126.57 126.55 126.53
Fastest Lap	M. Dunlop (Yamaha)	128.60
Supersport 600cc (B)		
1st 2nd 3rd	K. Amor (Honda) I. Hutchinson (Honda) W. Dunlop (Yamaha)	126.31 126.29 126.25
Fastest Lap	K. Amor (Honda)	128.46
Supertwins		
1st 2nd 3rd	R. Farquhar (Kawasaki) J. Burrows (Kawasaki) R. McCartney (Kawasaki)	115.44 110.87 110.36
Fastest Lap	R. Farquhar (Kawasaki)	116.68
250cc		
1st 2nd 3rd	I. Lougher (Honda) W. Dunlop (Honda) P. Robinson (Honda)	118.77 117.89 116.24
Fastest Lap	I. Lougher (Honda)	120.12
125cc		
1st 2nd 3rd	W. Dunlop (Honda) P. Robinson (Honda) S. Dunlop (Honda)	107.91 107.48 103.72
Fastest Lap	W. Dunlop (Honda)	109.16
Classic		
1st 2nd 3rd	O. Linsdell (Paton) N. McWhirter (Norton) M. McGaw (Seeley Weslake)	110.00 102.13 101.33
Fastest Lap	O. Linsdell (Paton)	111.64

2011 11 & 13 August

Superbike (A)		
1st 2nd 3rd	B. Anstey (Honda) G. Martin (Suzuki) K. Amor (Honda)	130.53 129.92 129.90
Fastest Lap	B. Anstey (Honda)	131.88
Superbike (B)		
1st 2nd 3rd	G. Martin (Suzuki) K. Amor (Honda) W. Dunlop (Honda)	128.16 127.86 127.85
Fastest Lap	W. Dunlop (Honda)	130.50
Superstock		
1st 2nd 3rd	M. Dunlop (Kawasaki) G. Martin (Suzuki) G. Johnson (Honda)	124.94 124.77 123.81
Fastest Lap	M. Dunlop (Kawasaki)	128.98
Supersport 600cc (A)		
1st 2nd 3rd	M. Dunlop (Yamaha) W. Dunlop (Honda) B. Anstey (Honda)	125.49 125.45 125.40
Fastest Lap	B. Anstey (Honda)	128.06
Supersport 600cc (B)		
1st 2nd 3rd	M. Dunlop (Yamaha) W. Dunlop (Honda) C. Donald (Honda)	126.62 126.54 126.48
Fastest Lap	M. Dunlop (Yamaha)	128.20

Supertwins		
1st 2nd 3rd	R. Farquhar (Kawasaki) A. Archibald (Kawasaki) J. Burrows (Kawasaki)	112.57 107.67 107.63
Fastest Lap	R. Farquhar (Kawasaki)	114.10
250cc		
1st 2nd 3rd	I. Lougher (Honda) D. Robb (Honda) J. Coward (Honda)	109.28 108.74 108.17
Fastest Lap	S. Elliott (Honda)	112.03
125cc		
1st 2nd 3rd	I. Lougher (Honda) P. Robinson (Aprilia) S. Dunlop (Honda)	100.95 100.01 96.80
Fastest Lap	P. Robinson (Aprilia)	102.61
Classic		
1st 2nd 3rd	O. Linsdell (Royal Enfield) M. McGaw (Seeley Weslake) P. Coward (Honda)	96.52 93.06 93.05
Fastest Lap	O. Linsdell (Royal Enfield)	98.30

2012 **9 & 11 August**

Superbike (A)		
1st 2nd 3rd	G. Martin (Suzuki) G. Johnson (Honda) C. Cummins (Suzuki)	131.45 130.94 130.17
Fastest Lap	M. Dunlop (Honda)	133.26
Superbike (B)		
1st 2nd 3rd	M. Dunlop (Honda) G. Martin (Suzuki) C. Cummins (Suzuki)	132.00 131.96 130.67
Fastest Lap	M. Dunlop (Honda)	133.43
Superstock		
1st 2nd 3rd	M. Dunlop (Kawasaki) I. Lougher (Kawasaki) G. Martin (Suzuki)	129.50 129.08 128.95
Fastest Lap	M. Dunlop (Kawasaki)	131.53

Supersport 600cc (A)		
1st 2nd 3rd	W. Dunlop (Honda) B. Anstey (Honda) L. Johnston (Honda)	125.61 125.58 124.35
Fastest Lap	W. Dunlop (Honda)	127.31
Supersport 600cc (B)		
1st 2nd 3rd	B. Anstey (Honda) W. Dunlop (Honda) C. Cummins (Suzuki)	126.49 126.47 125.40
Fastest Lap	B. Anstey (Honda)	127.95
Supertwins		
1st 2nd 3rd	R. Farquhar (Kawasaki) J. Hamilton (Kawasaki) R. Mountford (Kawasaki)	116.97 114.45 113.82
Fastest Lap	R. Farquhar (Kawasaki)	118.46
250cc		
1st 2nd 3rd	D. Morgan (Honda) S. Elliott (Honda) K. Strowger (Honda)	113.17 111.00 110.09
Fastest Lap	D. Morgan (Honda)	114.79
125cc		
1st 2nd 3rd	W. Dunlop (Honda) S. Wilson (Honda) O. Linsdell (Honda)	109.44 109.03 106.50
Fastest Lap	W. Dunlop (Honda)	112.05

2013 **17 August**

Superbike (A)		
1st 2nd 3rd	G. Martin (Suzuki) M. Dunlop (Honda) W. Dunlop (Yamaha)	131.62 131.61 130.63
Fastest Lap	M. Dunlop (Honda)	133.13
Superbike (B)		
1st 2nd 3rd	G. Martin (Suzuki) B. Anstey (Honda) C. Cummins (Yamaha)	131.18 130.75 130.35
Fastest Lap	G. Martin (Suzuki)	132.93

Superstock		
1st 2nd 3rd	M. Dunlop (Honda) G. Johnson (Kawasaki) B. Anstey (Honda)	127.19 126.52 125.24
Fastest Lap	M. Dunlop (Honda)	130.10
Supersport 600cc (A)		
1st 2nd 3rd	G. Martin (Suzuki) B. Anstey (Honda) L. Johnston (Honda)	118.68 118.67 117.12
Fastest Lap	B. Anstey (Honda)	120.76
Supersport 600cc (B)		
1st 2nd 3rd	W. Dunlop (Yamaha) B. Anstey (Honda) C. Cummins (Yamaha)	126.35 126.34 125.25
Fastest Lap	W. Dunlop (Yamaha)	127.93
Supertwins		
1st 2nd 3rd	I. Lintin (Kawasaki) J. Hamilton (Kawasaki) L. Johnston (Kawasaki)	114.04 114.03 113.85
Fastest Lap	J. Hamilton (Kawasaki)	116.26
125cc		
1st 2nd 3rd	I. Lougher (Honda) C. Elkin (Honda) P. Jordan (Honda)	106.32 106.28 102.54
Fastest Lap	C. Elkin (Honda)	108.01

2014 **16 August**

Superbike		
1st 2nd 3rd	B. Anstey (Honda) G. Martin (Suzuki) L. Johnston (Honda)	128.25 128.23 127.83
Fastest Lap	B. Anstey (Honda)	131.89
Superstock		
1st 2nd 3rd	D. Kneen (Suzuki) D. Harrison (Kawasaki) B. Anstey (Honda)	123.26 123.26 123.25
Fastest Lap	B. Anstey (Honda)	125.30
Supersport 600cc		
1st 2nd 3rd	B. Anstey (Honda) L. Johnston (Honda) G. Martin (Suzuki)	123.83 123.21 122.05
Fastest Lap	B. Anstey (Honda)	126.08
Supertwins		
1st 2nd 3rd	I. Lintin (Kawasaki) D. McGee (Kawasaki) J. Cowton (Kawasaki)	108.47 107.21 106.45
Fastest Lap	I. Lintin (Kawasaki)	109.84
250cc		
1st 2nd 3rd	J. Cowton (Yamaha) J. Ella (Honda) I. Morrell (Yamaha)	103.02 100.66 99.09
Fastest Lap	J. Cowton (Yamaha)	104.31
125cc		
1st 2nd 3rd	D. Mathison (Honda) C. Elkin (Honda) P. Jordan (Honda)	101.92 101.90 98.59
Fastest Lap	D. Mathison (Honda)	104.85

2015 **8 August**

Superbike (A)		
1st 2nd 3rd	B. Anstey (Honda) I. Hutchinson (Kawasaki) L. Johnston (BMW)	131.31 131.25 131.20
Fastest Lap	I. Hutchinson (Kawasaki)	133.04
Superbike (B)		
1st 2nd 3rd	P. Hickman (BMW) C. Cummins (Honda) M. Dunlop (BMW)	118.14 118.13 118.01
Fastest Lap	C. Cummins (Honda)	120.90
Superstock		
1st 2nd 3rd	L. Johnston (BMW) P. Hickman (BMW) M. Dunlop (BMW)	131.20 131.19 130.49
Fastest Lap	L. Johnston (BMW)	132.79

Supersport 600cc (A)		
1st 2nd 3rd	L. Johnston (Triumph) W. Dunlop (Yamaha) G. Irwin (Kawasaki)	127.22 127.22 126.98
Fastest Lap	L. Johnston (Triumph)	128.91
Supersport 600cc (B)		
1st 2nd 3rd	L. Johnston (Triumph) G. Irwin (Kawasaki) I. Hutchinson (Yamaha)	125.33 125.25 125.22
Fastest Lap	L. Johnston (Triumph)	128.08
Supertwins		
1st 2nd 3rd	D. McGee (Kawasaki) J. Cowton (Kawasaki) D. Cooper (Kawasaki)	109.03 108.30 108.17
Fastest Lap	D. McGee (Kawasaki)	111.42
250cc		
1st 2nd 3rd	S. Wilson (Honda) N. Kernohan (Honda) J. Cowton (Yamaha)	113.57 112.69 111.90
Fastest Lap	S. Wilson (Honda)	115.57
125cc		
1st 2nd 3rd	C. Elkin (Honda) C. Behan (Honda) N. Moore (Honda)	106.97 104.59 104.57
Fastest Lap	C. Elkin (Honda)	108.17

2016 **13 August**

Superbike (A)		
1st 2nd 3rd	I. Hutchinson (BMW) B. Anstey (Honda) M. Dunlop (BMW)	132.52 132.49 132.23
Fastest Lap	P. Hickman (Kawasaki)	133.89
Superbike (B)		
1st 2nd 3rd	I. Hutchinson (BMW) B. Anstey (Honda) M. Dunlop (BMW)	132.38 132.29 132.23
Fastest Lap	I. Hutchinson (BMW)	134.09
Superstock		
1st 2nd 3rd	I. Hutchinson (BMW) M. Dunlop (BMW) D. Kneen (Yamaha)	130.43 130.40 129.70
Fastest Lap	I. Hutchinson (BMW)	132.29
Supersport 600cc (A)		
1st 2nd 3rd	B. Anstey (Honda) I. Hutchinson (Yamaha) C. Cummins (Honda)	125.10 124.98 124.60
Fastest Lap	I. Hutchinson (Yamaha)	128.51
Supersport 600cc (B)		
1st 2nd 3rd	I. Hutchinson (Yamaha) W. Dunlop (Yamaha) P. Hickman (Kawasaki)	126.48 126.47 126.43
Fastest Lap	P. Hickman (Kawasaki)	128.51
Supertwins		
1st 2nd 3rd	D. Cooper (Kawasaki) D. Sheils (Kawasaki) J. Cowton (Kawasaki)	115.29 115.24 115.22
Fastest Lap	P. Jordan (Kawasaki)	116.86
250cc		
1st 2nd 3rd	N. Kernohan (Honda) D. Morgan (Honda) D. Tweed (Kawasaki)	112.77 111.09 105.38
Fastest Lap	N. Kernohan (Honda)	113.86
125cc		
1st 2nd 3rd	C. Elkin (Honda) S. Wilson (Honda) P. Robinson (Honda)	106.61 104.84 104.55
Fastest Lap	C. Elkin (Honda)	107.58

2017 **12 August**

Superbike (A)		
1st 2nd 3rd	B. Anstey (Honda) P. Hickman (BMW) D. Harrison (Kawasaki)	133.18 133.15 133.08
Fastest Lap	D. Harrison (Kawasaki)	134.61

Superbike (B)		
1st 2nd 3rd	D. Harrison (Kawasaki) D. Kneen (BMW) C. Cummins (Honda)	132.09 132.08 132.05
Fastest Lap	D. Kneen (BMW)	133.64
Superstock		
1st 2nd 3rd	P. Hickman (BMW) D. Harrison (Kawasaki) D. Kneen (BMW)	131.10 130.60 130.59
Fastest Lap	P. Hickman (BMW)	132.77
Supersport 600cc (A)		
1st 2nd 3rd	P. Hickman (Triumph) B. Anstey (Honda) L. Johnston (Honda)	126.23 126.21 126.13
Fastest Lap	B. Anstey (Honda)	127.86
Supersport 600cc (B)		
1st 2nd 3rd	P. Hickman (Triumph) B. Anstey (Honda) L. Johnston (Honda)	126.83 126.80 126.74
Fastest Lap	B. Anstey (Honda)	127.94
Supertwins		
1st 2nd 3rd	I. Lintin (Kawasaki) D. Cooper (Kawasaki) A. McLean (Kawasaki)	119.01 119.01 116.70
Fastest Lap	I. Lintin (Kawasaki)	120.40
250cc		
1st 2nd 3rd	D. Morgan (Honda) P. Owen (Honda) C. Laidlaw (Yamaha)	111.56 111.14 110.69
Fastest Lap	N. Kernohan (Honda)	113.32
125cc		
1st 2nd 3rd	P. Robinson (Honda) C. Elkin (Honda) J. Thompson (Honda)	109.69 109.67 108.96
Fastest Lap	C. Elkin (Honda)	111.34

2018 **9 & 11 August**

Superbike		
1st 2nd 3rd	P. Hickman (BMW) L. Johnston (Honda) D. Johnson (BMW)	126.37 125.95 125.60
Fastest Lap	L. Johnston (Honda)	127.83
Superstock		
1st 2nd 3rd	D. Harrison (Kawasaki) P. Hickman (BMW) C. Cummins (Honda)	131.80 131.76 130.96
Fastest Lap	D. Harrison (Kawasaki)	133.83
Supersport 600cc (A)		
1st 2nd 3rd	C. Cummins (Honda) A. McLean (Kawasaki) D. Harrison (Kawasaki)	122.97 122.20 121.73
Fastest Lap	C. Cummins (Honda)	125.59
Supersport 600cc (B)		
1st 2nd 3rd	P. Hickman (Triumph) L. Johnston (Honda) C. Cummins (Honda)	126.97 126.18 126.17
Fastest Lap	P. Hickman (Triumph)	128.83
Supertwins		
1st 2nd 3rd	A. McLean (Kawasaki) C. Elkin (Kawasaki) I. Lougher (Kawasaki)	111.78 111.24 108.28
Fastest Lap	A. McLean (Kawasaki)	113.46
250cc (A)		
1st 2nd 3rd	N. Kernohan (Honda) S. Anderson (Honda) D. Tweed (Kawasaki)	110.87 110.12 108.22
Fastest Lap	N. Kernohan (Honda)	112.14
250cc (B)		
1st 2nd 3rd	S. Anderson (Honda) N. Kernohan (Honda) D. Tweed (Kawasaki)	104.98 103.54 103.01
Fastest Lap	S. Anderson (Honda)	107.03

125cc (A)		
1st 2nd 3rd	C. Elkin (Honda) M. Dokoupil (Ariane) N. Moore (Honda)	107.71 105.02 101.88
Fastest Lap	C. Elkin (Honda)	109.24
125cc (B)		
1st 2nd 3rd	M. Dokoupil (Ariane) C. Elkin (Honda) P. Robinson (Honda)	98.53 98.46 98.07
Fastest Lap	M. Dokoupil (Ariane)	98.53

2019 **8 & 10 August**

Superbike (A)		
1st 2nd 3rd	P. Hickman (BMW) D. Harrison (Kawasaki) C. Cummins (Honda)	133.30 132.36 131.84
Fastest Lap	P. Hickman (BMW)	136.41
Superbike (B)		
1st 2nd 3rd	P. Hickman (BMW) D. Harrison (Kawasaki) C. Cummins (Honda)	123.29 123.01 122.93
Fastest Lap	D. Harrison (Kawasaki)	126.32
Superbike (C)		
1st 2nd 3rd	P. Hickman (BMW) D. Harrison (Kawasaki) C. Cummins (Honda)	132.73 131.97 130.41
Fastest Lap	P. Hickman (BMW)	134.50
Superstock		
1st 2nd 3rd	P. Hickman (BMW) D. Todd (BMW) C. Cummins (Honda)	121.31 119.12 118.62
Fastest Lap	P. Hickman (BMW)	122.83
Supersport 600cc (A)		
1st 2nd 3rd	P. Hickman (Triumph) L. Johnston (Yamaha) D. Harrison (Kawasaki)	126.61 126.57 125.57
Fastest Lap	P. Hickman (Triumph)	127.93
Supersport 600cc (B)		
1st 2nd 3rd	P. Hickman (Triumph) L. Johnston (Yamaha) D. Todd (Honda)	117.98 117.11 116.92
Fastest Lap	P. Hickman (Triumph)	119.33
Supersport 600cc (C)		
1st 2nd 3rd	P. Hickman (Triumph) L. Johnston (Yamaha) C. Cummins (Honda)	124.58 124.57 123.00
Fastest Lap	P. Hickman (Triumph)	127.37
Supertwins (A)		
1st 2nd 3rd	P. Jordan (Kawasaki) J. Loughlin (Paton) J. Coward (Kawasaki)	117.77 117.76 117.73
Fastest Lap	J. Coward (Kawasaki)	119.48
Supertwins (B)		
1st 2nd 3rd	C. Elkin (Kawasaki) J. Loughlin (Paton) L. Johnston (Kawasaki)	114.29 114.28 113.18
Fastest Lap	J. Coward (Kawasaki)	116.00
250cc		
1st 2nd 3rd	N. Kernohan (Honda) D. Morgan (Honda) P. Williams (Yamaha)	111.60 111.59 108.03
Fastest Lap	D. Morgan (Honda)	112.91
125cc		
1st 2nd 3rd	M. Dokoupil (Ariane) C. Elkin (Honda) M. Kennedy (Honda)	107.43 107.20 102.49
Fastest Lap	M. Dokoupil (Ariane)	110.00

2020–22 **UGP cancelled due to a combination of financial difficulty and the coronavirus pandemic.**

APPENDIX 2
WINNERS

Wins	Rider
24	J. Dunlop
18	I. Lougher
14	P. McCallen
13	B. Anstey
	P. Hickman
11	G. Martin
9	R. Dunlop
	R. Farquhar
	I. Hutchinson
	B. Reid
7	G. Agostini
	W. Dunlop
	S.M.B. Hailwood
	B. Jackson
	R. McCullough
	S. Woods
6	M. Dunlop
	J. Surtees
	B. Swallow
	J.G. Williams
5	M. Cann
	W.L. Handley
	R. Haslam
	T. Herron
	E. Laycock
	D. Lindsay
	T. Rutter
	C. Ubbiali
4	A. Archibald
	J. Craig
	I. Duffus
	C. Elkin
	J. Griffiths
	D. Jefferies
	J. Redman
	L. Taveri
3	S. Cull
	L.H. Davenport
	G.E. Duke
	F.L. Frith
	G. Hocking
	R. Holden
	W. D. Ivy
	L. Johnston
	C. Junk
	N. Kernohan
	I. Lintin
	W.A. Lomas
	O. McNally
	P. Mellor
	E.A. Mellors
	P. Owens
	P.W. Read
	D. Robinson
	E.R. Thomas
	G.W. Walker
2	W.R. Amm
	H.R. Anderson
	F. Andrews
	M. Boddice
	K. Carruthers
	W.A. Colgan
	J. Cronshaw
	C. Cummins
	C.J.P. Dodson
	M. Dokoupil
	K. Enders
	R. Fisher
	C. Fogarty
	D. Gallagher
	W. Haas
	D. Harrison
	J. Hartle
	S. Hislop
	K.T. Kavanagh
	T. Keys
	O. Linsdell
	F.A. Longman
	W.A.C. McCandless
	J. McGuinness
	R. Marshall
	D. Morgan
	A. Nieto
	C.C. Sandford
	J.W. Shaw
	I. Simpson
	B. Smith
	J.M. West

Wins	Rider
1	K. Amor
	S. Anderson
	H.R. Armstrong
	G.M.R. Barry
	S. Beck
	A. J. Bell
	C. Bevan
	D. Brindley
	G. Brockerton
	J.G. Burney
	A. Buxton
	K.R. Campbell
	D. Cooper
	J. Courtney
	J. Cowton
	S.A. Crabtree
	P. Cranston
	R. Creith
	G. Crosby
	E. Degner
	A. de Gourley
	D. Edgington
	J. Ekerold
	J. Findlay
	A.R. Foster
	A. Geiss
	S. Gleave
	R.L. Graham
	J. Guthrie
	H.W. Hassall
	A. Hockley
	Y. Holland
	R. Hollaus
	K. Howles
	A. Jackson
	A. 'Bud' Jackson
	G. Jamison
	N. Jefferies
	P. Jordan
	D. Keen
	D. Kneen
	L. Liberati
	G. Lingham
	J. Lockett
	E. Lorenzetti
	D. McGee
	G. McGregor
	R. McIntyre
	A. McLean
	N. McWhirter
	L.G. Martin
	D. Mathison
	N.P. Metcalfe
	E. Mitchell
	G. Molloy
	D. Molyneux
	A. Moyce
	K.H. Mudford
	W. Noll
	G. E. Nott
	E.S. Oliver
	H. Owesle
	C. Palmer
	A. Patterson
	J.A. Porter
	T. Provini
	R. Quayle
	J. Rea
	T. Reid
	T.H. Robb
	M. Robinson
	N. Robinson
	P. Robinson
	C. Rodgers
	B. Ruffo
	W.F. Rusk
	W. Seawright
	D. Serafini
	J.H. Simpson
	C. Smith
	F. Šťastný
	T. Steele
	P.H. Tait
	K. Takahashi
	F.A. Taylor
	P. Thorne
	G. Tunstall
	N. Tuxworth
	H.G. Tyrell-Smith
	A. Walsh
	J. Weeden
	D. Welsh
	C.I. Williams
	P.J. Williams
	S. Wilson
	S. 'Ginger' Wood
	S. Woods

APPENDIX 3
LAP RECORD HOLDERS

Old Clady Circuit

Year	Rider	Machine	Time	Speed (mph)
1922	H. Langman	Scott	18m 42s	65.70
1923	J. Whalley	Douglas	17m 58s	68.46
1924	S. Woods	New Imperial	16m 55s	72.71
1925	A. Bennett	Norton	16m 07s	76.32
1927	S. Woods	Norton	15m 43s	78.26
1928	C.J.P. Dodson	Sunbeam	15m 03s	81.72
1929	G.W. Walker	Rudge	14m 56s	82.36
1930	J.H. Simpson	Norton	14m 32s	84.63
1931	S. Woods	Norton	13m 43s	89.67
1934	W.F. Rusk	Velocette	13m 21s	92.13
1935	J. Guthrie	Norton	12m 54s	95.35
1938	J.M. West	BMW	12m 26s	98.93
1939	D. Serafini	Gilera	12m 17.8s	100.03

New Clady Circuit

Year	Rider	Machine	Time	Speed (mph)
1947	A.J. Bell	Norton	10m 27s	94.79
1949	R.L. Graham	AJS	10m 06s	98.08
1950	G.E. Duke	Norton	9m 44s	101.77
1952	R.L. Graham	MV	9m 21s	105.94

Dundrod Circuit

Year	Rider	Machine	Time	Speed (mph)
1953	G.E. Duke &	Gilera		
	K.T. Kavanagh	Norton	4m 51.0s	91.74
1955	W.A. Lomas	Guzzi	4m 43.0s	94.34
1956	G.E. Duke	Gilera	4m 42.6s	94.47
1957	J. Surtees	MV	4m 39.0s	95.69
1959	J. Surtees	MV	4m 36.0s	96.73
1960	J. Surtees	MV	4m 28.8s	99.32
1962	S.M.B. Hailwood	MV	4m 27.0s	99.99

Year	Rider	Machine	Time	Speed (mph)
1963	S.M.B. Hailwood	MV	4m 23.6s	101.28
1966	S.M.B. Hailwood	Honda	4m 13.6s	105.03
1967	S.M.B. Hailwood	Honda	4m 09.6s	106.71
1969	G. Agostini	MV	4m 07.4s	107.66
1975	R. McCullough	Yamaha	4m 05.4s	108.57
1976	G.M.R. Barry	Yamaha	3m 52.6s	114.55
1977	J.G. Williams	Suzuki	3m 51.6s	115.04
1978	T. Herron	Yamaha	3m 44.2s	118.84
1980	J. Dunlop	Suzuki	3m 44.0s	118.95
1982	R. Marshall	Suzuki	3m 42.2s	119.91
1984	J. Dunlop	Honda	3m 40.9s	120.62
1986	J. Dunlop	Honda	3m 40.5s	120.83
1988	E. Laycock	Honda	3m 39.5s	121.39
1989	C. Fogarty	Honda	3m 39.06s	121.629
1990	S. Hislop	Honda	3m 35.36s	123.719
1994	J. Griffiths	Kawasaki	3m 31.30s	126.100
1999	D. Jefferies	Yamaha	3m 30.03s	126.858
2002	I. Lougher	Suzuki	3m 28.45s	127.820
2003	A. Archibald	Suzuki	3m 27.83s	128.201
2004	B. Anstey	Suzuki	3m 26.481s	129.038
2006	I. Hutchinson	Kawasaki	3m 23.655s	130.829
2009	I. Hutchinson	Honda	3m 19.981s	133.232
2010	B. Anstey	Suzuki	3m 18.870s	133.977
2016	I. Hutchinson	BMW	3m 18.704s	134.089
2017	D. Harrison	Kawasaki	3m 17.928s	134.614
2019	P. Hickman	BMW	3m 15.316s	136.413

APPENDIX 4

LAP RECORDS

Old Clady Circuit

Class	Rider	Machine	Year	Time	Speed (mph)
500cc	D. Serafini	Gilera	1939	12m 17.8s	100.03
350cc	E.A. Mellors	Velocette	1939	13m 09s	93.54
250cc	E.R. Thomas	DKW	1938	14m 34s	84.44

New Clady Circuit

Class	Rider	Machine	Year	Time	Speed (mph)
500cc	R.L. Graham	MV	1952	9m 21s	105.94
350cc	G.E. Duke	Norton	1951	10m 04s	98.40
250cc	B. Ruffo	Moto Guzzi	1951	11m 05s	89.37
125cc	C. Ubbiali	Mondial	1950	12m 33s	78.92

Dundrod Circuit

Class	Rider	Machine	Year	Time	Speed (mph)
Superbike	P. Hickman	BMW	2019	3m 15.316s	136.413
Superstock	D. Harrison	Kawasaki	2018	3m 19.081s	133.835
Supersport	L. Johnston	Triumph	2015	3m 26.681s	128.913
Supertwin	I. Lintin	Kawasaki	2017	3m 41.292s	120.402
500cc	J. Dunlop	Honda	1984	3m 40.9s	120.62
400cc	C. Laidlaw	Yamaha	2017	3m 57.323s	112.269
350cc	B. Reid	Yamaha	1990	3m 47.0s	117.36
250cc	D. Lindsay	Honda	2006	3m 38.634s	121.866
200cc	N. Tuxworth	Yamaha	1976	4m 45.8s	93.23
Moto 3	C. Elkin	Honda	2017	3m 59.296s	111.343
125cc	W. Dunlop	Honda	2009	3m 55.017s	113.370
50cc	Á. Nieto	Derbi	1970	5m 17.2s	83.95
TT F1	J. Dunlop	Honda	1990	3m 36.7s	122.94
TT F2	B. Reid	Yamaha	1985	3m 54.0s	113.86
TT F3	R. Haslam	Honda	1980	4m 30.0s	98.68
Sidecars	K. Howles	Yamaha	1996	4m 00.7s	110.68

APPENDIX 5

RACE OFFICIALS

Chief Marshals

1922–1923	W.J. Chambers
	George Bowman

Clerks of the Course

1924	Thomas McGee
1925–31	Harry Palmer
1932–39	Malcolm Wilson
1947–56	Malcolm Wilson
1957–64	David Jennings
1965–71	Bertie Mann
1973–84	Kevin Martin
1985–89	Bertie Hunt
1990	Andrew Campbell
1991–92	Bertie Hunt
1993	Drew Armstrong
1994–2001	Billy Nutt
2002–19	Noel Johnston

APPENDIX 6
PROMOTERS AND SPONSORS

Race Promoters

1922–39	Ulster Motor Cycle Club
1947–62	Ulster Motor Cycle Club
1963	MCUI (Ulster Centre)
1964–71	Ulster Centre Promotions
1973–93	Ulster Centre Promotions
1994–2001	Coleraine & District Motor Club
2002–19	Dundrod & District Motorcycle Club

Main Event Sponsors

1965–66	Gallaher Ltd
1978–81	MacNaughton Blair Ltd
1983	Prentice
1984–85	Finlay
1986	Shell Oils
1987–88	BBC Radio Ulster
1989–90	Guinness
1993	Pepsi
1994–97	Coleraine / Ballymena / Belfast Plant Hire Ltd
1998–2000	CP Hire Ltd
2001–04	Stannifer Snoddons
2005	Northern Ireland Events
2006	Lisburn City Council
2007–08	Belfast Telegraph
2009	Stoneyford Concrete
2010–12	McKinstry Skip Hire Ltd
2013–15	Metzeler
2016–18	MCE Insurance
2019	fonaCAB

APPENDIX 7

FICM GRAND PRIX D'EUROPE

From 1924, until the Motorcycling World Championship was established in 1949, the FICM each year selected one of the Grands Prix to be designated as the Grand Prix d'Europe. The Ulster Grand Prix was accorded this honour on two occasions: 1935 and 1948. In fact, the 1948 race at Clady was the last event to carry the title.

Year	Grand Prix selected	Circuit
1924	Italian GP	Monza
1925	Italian GP	Monza
1926	Belgian GP	Spa-Francorchamps
1927	German GP	Nürburgring
1928	Swiss GP	Meyrin
1929	Spanish GP	Granollers
1930	Belgian GP	Spa-Francorchamps
1931	French GP	Montlhéry
1932	Italian GP	Littorio
1933	Swedish GP	Saxtorp
1934	Dutch TT	Assen
1935	Ulster GP	Clady
1936	German GP	Sachsenring
1937	Swiss GP	Bremgarten
1938	German GP	Sachsenring
1939	Belgian GP	Spa-Francorchamps
1947	Swiss GP	Bremgarten
1948	Ulster GP	Clady

APPENDIX 8
IN MEMORIAM

Riders

1926	Ted Stuart	350cc Coventry Eagle
1928	J.C. Allen	500cc Norton
1936	Ben Bickell	500cc Ariel
1951	Gianni Leoni	250cc Moto-Guzzi
1951	Sante Geminiani	500cc Moto-Guzzi
1952	Norman Stewart	350cc Norton
1955	Julian Crossley	350cc AJS
1956	Derek Ennett	350cc Moto-Guzzi
1961	Ron Miles	500cc Norton
1977	John Molyneux	Sidecar Kawasaki
1977	George Oates	Sidecar Kawasaki
1978	Jeremy Swann	500cc Suzuki
1978	John Williams	750cc Yamaha
1986	Stephen Smyth	350cc Yamaha
1987	Klaus Klein	750cc Yamaha
1992	Steve Johnson	250cc Yamaha
1995	Martin Murphy	Sidecar Yamaha
1997	Steven Galligan	Sidecar Yamaha
1999	Owen McNally	250cc Aprilia
2002	Gary Jess	1000cc Yamaha
2004	Andy Wallace	1000cc Suzuki
2015	Andy Lawson	600cc Kawasaki
2018	Fabrice Miguet	1000cc Kawasaki

Non-riders

1961	Albert Walters	Marshal
1977	Jane Cardwell	Spectator
1997	Christopher McConnell-Hewitt	Spectator
2001	Gerald Allaway	Flag marshal

'Bike Week' Dundrod 150

2012	Lee Vernon	1000cc BMW
2017	Jamie Hodson	600cc Yamaha
2017	Gavin Lupton	600cc Honda

ACKNOWLEDGEMENTS

I would like to place on record my sincere thanks to all who assisted me in the task of producing this book. Most of the photographs from the earlier years of the race are from the archives of *Motor Cycle Weekly*, and were given to me many years ago by the then editor, Mick Woollett. Others were supplied by W.A. Martin and Bertie Martin, who are sadly no longer with us, Bill Snelling of FoTTofinder Bikesport Archives, Derek McIntyre, as well as Clifford McClean/Pacemaker Press, and John Tennant.

The vast majority of the more recent photographs were provided by four of my friends, to whom I am greatly indebted. They are Malcolm Donnellan, Alastair McCook, Eddie Mateer and Rowland White. It is true to say that without their unstinted help this book would have been well-nigh impossible. My grateful thanks to them all.

I would also like to acknowledge the assistance given to me by all at Blackstaff Press, especially Patsy Horton, Michelle Griffin, and Jacky Hawkes. All my idiosyncrasies were treated with patience and understanding, and it was a joy to renew my association with the press after so many years.

I am also extremely grateful to my wife, Jean, who for over half a century has put up with me going AWOL on race weekends without a murmur of complaint. Finally, I would like to acknowledge the support I have received from my daughter, Helen, and from my son, Philip, to whom I introduced the delights of road racing a long time ago, only to watch with envy as he became far more knowledgeable about it all.

Seventy-five years on from my first Ulster Grand Prix, I still harbour a sense of gratitude towards my late uncle for taking me with him to Clady, and so it is entirely fitting that I dedicate this book to the memory of John Meredith.